Edward Pearce

THE QUIET RISE
of
JOHN MAJOR

Best wishes

Edward Pearce

WEIDENFELD AND NICOLSON
LONDON

Illustration Acknowledgments

The photographs in this book have been reproduced
by kind permission of: Alan Duncan 8, 9;
Gamma/Frank Spooner Pictures 11; Huntingdon
Conservative Party 5, 6, 7 above; John and Norma
Major 1, 2, 7 below, 12; Syndication International 10.

Published in Great Britain by
George Weidenfeld & Nicolson Limited
91 Clapham High Street
London SW4 7TA

ISBN 0 297 81208 4

Printed in Great Britain by Butler & Tanner Ltd,
Frome and London

Contents

Author's
Acknowledgements

As this book was written with the help of forty-five interviews with private citizens and cabinet ministers, friends, colleagues and opponents, specific acknowledgement would be invidious. The person who must be given unreserved thanks is my wife Deanna, who has corrected initial copy, printed from a less than helpful word processor, read proofs and compiled the index, making the word 'indispensable' an understatement.

In memory of my father,
Frank Pearce

From Longfellow Road

The future Prime Minister of Britain was born on 29 March 1943 in South London, the last child of Thomas Major-Ball and his second wife Gwendolin (née Coates). His mother was gravely ill during the pregnancy with double pneumonia and pleurisy. According to her elder son Terry, both she and the baby nearly died. Within a year a V2 rocket landed near enough to blow out windows and spatter his cot with fragments. On her own insistence his mother took John and the other children for a year to a village in Norfolk.

The family's roots were in the West Midlands. The Prime Minister's grandfather was Abraham Ball of Bloxwich near Walsall. Abraham Ball was a master bricklayer who would spend an important part of his life in the United States. He obtained commissions which took him to a number of towns and cities in Pennsylvania building blast furnaces for the Carnegie steel mills. When his wife Sarah, also from the West Midlands, fell pregnant in the US, she was sent home for the child to be born in England. That child, christened Abraham Thomas, was born at New Street, Bloxwich on 18 May 1879. Abraham Thomas was taken back to America and spent his childhood there in Pennsylvania, from, his son Terry thinks, roughly 1880 to 1895 when there is a record of him being back in Walsall. Tom, as he was known, stayed in the area for a while working at his father's trade as he had done in the States, but disliking, as Terry reports, the ferociously dirty labour of scraping brick-wall surfaces and burning out paint cans for re-use.

He was physically strong, a gymnast, and represented local swimming and water-polo teams. He had also played baseball as a junior in America and learned baton-throwing with a brass band in Philadelphia. His name as a swimmer disappears from local newspapers around 1900 and shortly after begins to appear in theatrical bills. His variety of skills enabled him to function as juggler and acrobat (the family have his trapeze artist's costume), but also as patter-comedian, who sang and dabbled in song writing. He appears to have functioned in the theatre either as a variety act with an artiste who would later become his first wife Kitty, Drum and Major, (an echo of his American experience as a boy drum major?) or as the manager of a review or concert party, a travelling bill taking theatres for their own show. This is the world of J. B. Priestley's *Good Companions*. Tom's concert parties had various names, one of which is recorded as 'Special Edition'. He would tell his son that in a career of nearly thirty years on stage from 1901, he didn't think there was a theatre in England, Scotland, Wales or Ireland he hadn't played. But his base in England from 1911 was a house in Higher Heath near Whitchurch, Shropshire.

The party also toured abroad, theatrical papers recording their return from a year in South America. At some stage of this tour he found himself in the middle of a local rising. A local official confused by the name 'Major' (aren't we all?) took him for a British officer and put him in charge of a group of militiamen. Tom splendidly distinguished by a white armband, took them outside the town, disbanded them, got his passport and slipped away.

The first marriage to his stage partner, celebrated in 1910, had been childless. Tom would lose his first wife Kitty, five years older than himself, through a stage accident when a steel girder supporting a fire curtain came loose, struck her on the head and inflicted grave head injuries from which, after a year, she died in 1928.

Tom Major's second wife, and John's mother, Gwendolin Coates, was a speciality dancer in a two-girl act called 'Glade and Glen'. Since the other girl was called Gladys, she must have been Glade, and Gwen Coates will have been Glen. There was an age gap between her and Tom Major at the time of their marriage in 1929. Born in 1906 she was twenty-seven years younger. Terry reports a family belief that Gwen Coates had been close to Kitty who in the event of predisease had wanted her to marry the distraught Tom. The children of this marriage were a premature baby, Thomas Aston born 20 June 1929 but dying the same day, Patricia June born 3 June 1930 at Gainsborough, Terry Major (so given) 2 July 1932 at Old Maldon Surrey and John Roy in Carshalton on 29 March 1943.

The name Major was one which Tom had taken at an early stage in his theatrical career (though he is billed at one point as Tom Drum). He liked Major but piled Pelion on to the Ossa of this muddle by being known also as Major-Ball. This, Gwen seems to have disliked. For whatever reason, the recorded surnames of the family are confusing. Terry was registered as Ball (surname), Terry Major (christian names). John appears as Major (surname), John Roy (christian names). A combination of theatre people's pseudonyms and a certan grandeur towards literary accuracy has started a number of hares, all of which should be left to escape. John Roy Major, not a member of the theatrical profession, has been John Roy Major from birth.

John Major's recollection of his mother is tender. 'Physically she was slight,' he says, 'about five foot four, slender and supple.' She was 'a very considerable home maker, throwing a girdle round her family, keeping everyone in and, more to the point, keeping others out.' She did though, 'have a tremendous capacity for discovering and encouraging lame ducks of every kind. You would find them in the kitchen. If she found a lame duck you could be sure she would befriend that person and we would see a great deal of them.'

Home in John's childhood was Longfellow Road, Worcester Park, Surrey, a pleasant, comfortable area doomed to be called suburban. The children played in the street, John among them, remembered by a friend, in a thorn-brown patterned pullover, a little way up the street in front of a block of three lock-up garages in a space known as Tilbury's Yard. It was good for cricket and football but if the ball went too far you had to climb over a spiked gate to get it back. John Major, like his friends, attended Cheam Common Primary and Junior schools where the Headmistress was Mrs Wood.

One of those friends, Alan Carpenter, now a builder in Epsom, identifies the group of 'football and cricket mad' children, girls included, followed everywhere by Alan's little dog, who took part in these games. 'There was Laurie Sargent and his sister Wendy, Anthony Scott, Eddie and Maureen Golightly (next door to the Majors), Bobby Archer and John Brand, all of whose families lived on that road.' One recollection of Alan's concerns a fierce resentful woman called Mrs Bates who, if the ball went into her garden would keep it unless one of two polite boys, himself or John Major, went and asked for it very nicely.

Gwen Major's kindness and charity survived the fall in the family's fortunes. In 1933 Tom Major had gone into business after his Bohemian theatrical travels. Learning the essentials of clay model-ling and moulding, which he would later teach his sons, he made garden goods – vases, birdtables and ornaments – and for a while satisfactorily traded as Major's Garden Ornaments. For much of this time he was working out of his own garage. Alan Carpenter recalls an elderly man in brown corduroy trousers, his hair swept back and on the long side, and the whole of him covered with dust, who came, went and worked in his open garage. His elder children, Terry and Pat, also worked for him, and for considerable periods, so did employed workers and there were other workshops, one of them in Surbiton. His business card also describes him as a dealer in balast and other builders' materials. It was for some time a busy little undertaking. But business was stopped by the War and during it Tom, whose sight was deteriorating but who functioned as an air raid warden, had had a near fatal fall on stairs, hitting his chest above the heart on the rim of his warden's steel helmet.

The business finally went wrong several years after the War when he had an access of capital from a woman who withdrew her support after that money had gone into expansion, notably into new premises near Worcester Park Station. Tom, already registered as blind and well over seventy, was threatened with legal proceedings and driven to meet a body of debt which was to cause his children considerable grief. The family was obliged to sell the home to meet the debt, and moved in May 1955, when John was twelve and already at Rutlish Grammar School, from the comfort of Worcester Park to the bleak-ness of Coldharbour Lane, Brixton. That was a ferocious move down with an impact on the youngest boy which can only be guessed at.

But the reflexive kindness of Gwendolin Major – charity is altogether the wrong word – survived the fall in fortune. She kept this up for 'people out of work, widowed people, those with some physical or mental problems, almost to the time she died.' Her son recalls that she seemed to have 'a natural affinity for the underdog; she would invite them in, always using the kitchen for such hospitality. The kettle would be boiling and they would be there.' But her health began to deteriorate. Asthma and chronic bronchitis would turn mortally into emphysema.

There was no politics in the home. Tom and Gwen's younger son is reasonably sure that they were Conservative voters, 'if only out of admiration for Winston Churchill,' but he has no recollection of party politics being discussed in the household. The one political argument he recalls was with his father and related to race. Tom Major had spent some time in America around the turn of the century. American piety on racial equality is a recent bloom. A reflexive contempt for 'negroes' or 'boys' of the kind depicted in the novel *Ragtime* was widespread until well into the late fifties. Consequently his father's attitudes, affected by American assumptions, 'were a bit harder than mine; so we disagreed about that.'

John Major cannot recall a time when he has not held to his firm dislike of racial discrimination, but as he says, 'it isn't any different to the dislike I have for patronizing attitudes generally, the belief that some people are better than others by an accident of birth or events.' Dislike of racialism was 'only that attitude writ large.' Incidentally, he denies having a prejudice against the upper classes. 'It's easy to misread me here.' But he does feel 'a rooted dislike of patronizing attitudes and bigotry.'

His experience of school was mixed. At eleven he had won a scholarship under the old 11-plus system to Rutlish Grammar school in Wimbledon. Alan Carpenter says that he knew no other boy from the area who went so far away. It was by John's account neither a cruel nor brutal establishment. 'There were no great beasts in the place.' But it seems to have been stiff and strict, perhaps touched with that urge to be a mimic public school which so often counterpointed the academic good sense of the grammar schools. The happy memories are of sport, cricket and, at this time, rugby, to which he was introduced by the deputy head 'Bobby' Oulton. Playing centre at first, he was moved to full back when it was noticed that he was a quite resolute tackler.

He had a single mentor from the school, remembered with great affection, Harry Hathaway, the maths teacher. A former AAA time keeper, he was 'in many ways a Mr Chips of the fifties. A bachelor, lived for his boys, cared a great deal about them, quite strict, quite severe, but would go to any lengths at all to protect them against anyone else and to teach them. He was the very best sort of school teacher.' (By a happy chance when, almost twenty years later, John Major was the Conservative candidate for St Pancras North, a Mrs Pollard who came in to help at the Committee rooms, turned out to be Harry Hathaway's sister.)

Cricket, notoriously a passion of the Prime Minister, occupied a good deal of the schoolboy's time, but he denies being as good as some reports which have suggested he may have been close to county standard. 'Perhaps up to Club and Ground on my very best days,' is how he puts it. He 'would have *liked* to have been a professional cricketer, but was never good enough. Someone,' he says, 'is being kind in retrospect.' He 'got a few wickets, seven for nine, including a hat trick, against Royal Masonic.' The weakness in his batting was on the leg side, which for what it is worth, is, to the right-handed batsman, his left.

Scholastically, though, he insists on having worked up a dedicated idleness, though he had distinct preferences. 'I was bored beyond endurance by the sciences, I must say. I liked English, I *loved* History, I quite liked Maths and I much enjoyed Economic History. On the good subjects I suppose I did a modicum of work. When I did any work at all I did quite well. Mostly I didn't.' He is in earnest about lack of drive. 'I really didn't work is the truth. I really didn't do any work at all. It was almost a badge of honour not to in a curious way. I can't rationalize it. I wasn't troublesome. I didn't beat up the class. I just withdrew.' John Major cannot rationalize his attitude. That seems perhaps good reason for no one else to.

But for his early school-leaving (at sixteen) there is an underlying non-rationalized occasion. And, perhaps more obliquely, it helps account for his low effort. There is no mystery about the reasons why this highly intelligent person, widely credited ever since with photographic recall and flip-wristed mastery of a brief, did not stay for A levels, university entrance and the manifest destiny of Oxbridge. The Majors were poor, very poor.

The failed business and its debts hung upon them. It was nobody's fault, a great deal of hard work had been done, and businesses do fail. Both elder Majors are recalled as excellent parents, deeply concerned to provide everything for their last child as for John's elder brother and sister. It may have been this care and anxious trouble-taking which most motivated John Major to prefer making a living. Rutlish went in for handsome compulsory blazers with elaborate gilt buttons. He knew that his blazer was paid for out of the school fund, he knew that his mother had secured another old blazer at a jumble sale so that she could snip off the buttons which, new, cost half a crown each. His elder brother Terry recalls leaving the digs he had been living in to sleep at the workshop where he worked. Money which John might earn would make some contribution to the household. It would add something to sacrifices his brother and sister were already making.

One doesn't over-psychologize in pointing out that a working, prize-collecting, top-of-the-form pupil would be urgently kept at the school and university mill for five more years at least. A boy who has heard other people meaning to be kind, but whispering about the blazer, the buttons and the general need, carries a burden. His much older brother and sister carried another one and he has been anxious lately not to talk about the subject since it involves *their* deprivations and sacrifices. The Prime Minister's reticence on this subject should cause no surprise. It should start no further, less kind, whispering about non-existent mysteries.

His first earnings from Price Forbes, clerking in the City, were divided between family contributions, bus fares and 'paying for my first ill-fitting suit. It was, naturally, grey.' But he was able to do rather more for the family by leaving this desk job for a manual one with Davids' Rural Industries, a firm in business along similar lines to Tom Major's old business. Indeed its head, a retired naval commander whom Terry Ball remembers with affection, actually took over what was left of Major's Garden Ornaments and provided continued work for Terry and later John.

In his completed application form for the Huntingdon prospective candidacy Major refers to years spent as an 'industrial sculptor'. I had taken this to be an irony of some refinement alluding to his time on building sites when he was often employed mixing cement. In fact for two years he did sculpt as well as mould objects. Davids' were makers of everything from gnomes to ceremonial urns. John Major had learned the main techniques from his brother Terry and is rather proud of his skills. 'We didn't just turn out other people's moulds, we made our own models. Terry was better at it than I was, and my sister even more than him. Even today if you hand me a lump of clay, I will make you something rather good *and* make a mould out of it.'

At this time he lived with his brother at Burton Road, Brixton. They would get up very early, cycle down to the yard and work for a couple of hours mixing cement and turning out garden ornaments from the moulds before making off for the large transport café for breakfast – double beans on toast and more – 'the biggest breakfasts I've ever eaten.' Various fallacies and false legends must be cleared from the record about the Prime Minister, talk of food indicates one of them. Mr Major is categorical that contrary to several newspaper reports, he is neither an eater of exceptionally hot Vindaloo-in-spades curries, nor, despite the admiring devotion of the New Delhi Restaurant and Takeaway in Huntingdon, someone who eats curry every night. He quite likes it but he is no curry freak.

Another, perhaps more important legend should also be dispelled. The idea exists that between leaving school and somehow magically becoming a Young Conservative in a suit who worked in a bank, he simply drifted in a trance, a sort of James Dean rebel of inarticulate unpurpose, in and out of work by chance and whim. Real life involved no such attitudinizing. There were, apart from a few weeks on building sites, Price Forbes in the City, a couple of years at Davids' Rural Industries slapping clay into the 1960s' equivalents of the Infant Samuels and Garibaldis adorning Mole's courtyard, a specific period of unemployment and, finally, a job with the Electricity Board at the Elephant and Castle before his first banking job with the District Bank.

The unemployment had nothing of the rebel or the drop-out about it. By 1960 his father, now over eighty, was dying, and his mother chanced to be quite ill at the same time. It was agreed by the three siblings that John, as the youngest and the one earning least, should be the one to give up work to look after them. So he gave up his job at Davids' Rural Industries and did just that. Within a fairly short period Tom Major had died and Gwendolin had made a recovery. He was free to go back to work. But there was no job to be had. David's had eventually closed and despite the relative buoyancy of the times, he was refused work at a succession of interviews and given very little doubt that he was seen as someone who, having left steady employment, was clearly unreliable. He found it depressing to go to the Employment Office as it was then called and join a queue and find no work.

He has a recollection of watching Burt Lancaster in *Flame and the Arrow* for a shilling at the old Brixton Grand. There are Conservative politicians who will ripple with scarlet rage when talking of people like their new leader. Actually, work was seriously, not to say desperately, sought, but he was out of work nine months before a job came up from an Electricity Board willing to believe in his good faith and probable soundness.

But Major, whatever the glitches of his life so far, was not drifting. Why after all did he seek a job in banking? Because he says, emphatically, it was the one place where he could study and get a qualification without going away to college or accepting the articles and reduced earnings of other sorts of professional training. The wish for a political career had been there since he was thirteen. 'But I didn't at first connect the way I worked with that wish until a little later.' Circumstance immediately after leaving school 'trapped me a bit for a while until I could drag myself into a position where I could join the bank.' It took a while but 'I knew that either for business or a parliamentary seat I would need a qualification.' He would in fact work for and pass the examinations of the Institute of Banking.

Life at the District Bank which gave him his first banking job, apart from learning about bills, touring various departments and learning the rudiments, centred upon gaining his associateship of the Institute of Banking. He was now able to study in the morning very early, work at the bank during the day and engage in Tory politics in the evening, a strenuous but rather pleasant life and nothing at all to do with drift.

He also wished to travel, never having been abroad, not even to the Isle of Wight, also to earn some money. After eighteen months with the District Bank, he took up in mid 1965 a post with the more abroad-minded Standard Bank of West Africa. Known later as the Standard Charter Bank, it was the enterprise with which he was destined to be associated for many years. Six months after joining them, he volunteered for a posting to Nigeria where the civil war was just beginning and he arrived at Kano airport in early December 1966. Almost all of his recollections of that short period are happy and suggest a post-colonial version of Kipling–Maugham overseas pleasantness. An article printed in a local paper, *The Guardian* (Jos), on 24 December 1990 records the endearing if slightly vivid re-collections of Moses Dewa who acted as steward to the expatriates. Mr Dewa, well remembered by Major, describes the new junior official as 'a huge man from a wealthy family' and also as 'wearing an ash-coloured suit' which is a different way of saying the usual thing about him. Mr Dewa also recalls a teetotaler whose favourite meal at the local club was one of potatoes, beans and carrots.

He was in Jos, in the hill country of Northern Nigeria, three thousand feet up, a sort of African Simla: 'absolutely idyllic, I had fallen on my feet. You couldn't have been anywhere nicer.' He shared 'a rather special bachelor flat' with a young man from Liver-pool called Richard Cockeram who had a brand-new Cortina, 'the cause of our subsequent downfall.' He worked in the bank as one of a number of assistant accountants, getting up at five in the morning, listening to records on an old record player (most spare money went on records at this time). He remembers sitting there at 6 a.m. looking at 'the biggest, tallest skies I've ever seen,' then walking a mile to work every day after the eggs on toast served by Moses Dewa. At the weekends they would go to the Jos Club 'for a meal and the pleasure of just lounging around.'

His lack of racial feeling was gratefully noted. One African employee, Victor Kofoworola Lanyia, recalls from those days of *de facto* racial distinction when the Jos Club was for Europeans only, Major's insistence that Victor, who expected to have Europeans call him by his first name, should call him John. A bank messenger, Jostock Kilba, describes Major in the sad humble way of some subordinate people, as someone 'very hardworking, punctual, friendly to even people like us and was never over-bearing.' Moses

Dewa, who speaks of Major's humility, also recalls that if he was home ahead of a servant he would do some of his work. When Moses knocked at the bedroom door at 6.30 a.m. Major would answer at once, being already up. Dewa recalls Major's total failure to lose his temper, his abstinence from tobacco, non attendance at Church and the absence of any involvement with girls. Victor Lanyia, to whom he had mentioned unemployment and past problems, speaks of him as 'a man who behaved like one who had been schooled in a bitter experience with a grasp of the lessons taught'.

The accident which would bring him out of Africa occurred in May 1967 after a very happy six months. He and Richard Cockeram had been to watch a film; Cockeram had been drinking nothing stronger than Coca Cola. This call, according to the Jos *Guardian* was at another European club, the Yelwa. But by some piece of malignancy near Bukuru, a suburb of Jos, they drove half off a bluff. Major is fairly sure that he must actually have gone through the windscreen, and in addition to the well-known fact of losing his knee-cap, he suffered multiple fractures to the same left leg. (The Jos *Guardian* speaks of compound fractures of ankle and thigh as well as the knee injury.) He also has bad scarring beneath his chin though it lies out of reach of the cartoonists. 'There were other cuts, abrasions and minor fractions but I think I was jolly lucky to be alive.'

'I remember coming to, stretched out on this bank. Richard was beside me obviously in a state of shock, my trousers were cut to ribbons, another reason for thinking I went through the windscreen, and there was a fair amount of blood. But I couldn't move and I remember very plainly thinking "I've done it this time."' He kept thinking, 'I can't move. I've done it this time,' and mercifully kept blacking out. He recalls a local wagon coming by and being helped on to it. Then he woke up, his leg in traction, in a small operating theatre in an African mission hospital. (It was in fact Our Lady of Apostles on the Zaria By-Pass.) It was explained to him that he had suffered many fractures but also that the hospital, perhaps the equivalent of a cottage hospital here, had only rather old equipment.

He was there very briefly before being moved to Lagos where his bank arranged to fly him back to England and the Mayday hospital Croydon for long hospitalization and a series of operations. Apparently at one stage in his hospitalization amputation was at least considered. But in fact physiotherapy at St George's, Hyde Park, helped see him through. As it is, he is only discreetly handicapped but walking further than a mile is too much for him.

The Prime Minister recalls with gratitude the conduct of the bank. He was out of action for more than a year but not only did they keep him on, they gave him any rises that might have been coming, and somebody from the bank came to visit him every two weeks. 'I was treated supremely well even though I had been there only a few months and this was a civil accident. I have a great affection for them. I had been invalided for well over a year, so that on returning to work I was all skin and bone.' By the time of the 1968 London Borough election, he was still carrying a stick and hobbling around on it.

The time spent in hospital did however produce one single, huge, intangible advantage. Major had always been a reader, 'avaricious about print' is how he describes it. Moses Dewa remembers the economic and banking textbooks and the novels in his room. A year in hospital came in very helpful. It wasn't, he says, all improving. But as he read all of Jane Austen and most of Trollope (forty-nine novels), he was doing well enough. He expresses a strong preference for the Palliser sextet over the Barset novels, thus confirming the politician's preference shown by Harold Macmillan for a sequence of political novels over one of clerical conflict. He read 'a wide range of history and biography ... Oh, and a bit of cricket.' On the non-improving side, he read 'everything that Agatha Christie ever wrote.'

The habit continues and is long standing. He could not, even at school, bear to be bored standing round doing nothing, so I would always pick up a book.' And today he will get hold of a book once boxes are despatched last thing before going to sleep. For his banking exams he had read the standard textbooks of the day and – memo to dry zealots – 'got quite a long way with the *Wealth of Nations*' (at this he indicated a copy kept to hand in the Downing Street study). He is also a very keen collector of books.

Among his recurrent reading is 'embarrassingly' *Fame is the Spur* and *The Ragged Trousered Philanthropists*. Howard Spring's novel, based loosely on the life of Ramsay MacDonald, concerns a politician and his ambitions. Robert Tressell's work, always available at

Labour Party Conference book stalls, is a hunk of the socialist synoptic gospels, an account of the self-help of a group of building workers enjoying what might be called a high level of political consciousness. The fact that the Conservative Prime Minister has returned 'time and time again' to both says more for his candour and breadth of sympathy than the strongest admirers might have hoped.

The other recurring re-read is *Pride and Prejudice* 'which I went back to again and again as it is absolutely beautifully written.' Of the Palliser novels he likes *Phineas Finn* best of all, but with *The Prime Minister* whose Jewish semi-villain, Ferdinand Lopez, commits suicide in front of an express at Watford station, he was disappointed. A lacuna to which he admits is the European novel, having had his 'work cut out getting through English literature.'

Even without reading Proust, a discernible man had been rounded off. In a solid job, working at a professional qualification, somewhat travelled, suffering a big but survivable physical knock and now extensively read, a working draft of John Major now existed, fully ready for political life.

2

Lambeth Council

Jean Lucas is a pleasant woman in latish middle age. Now a councillor in the highly fashionable and successful borough of Wandsworth where the Tories have made themselves rather resplendently the flavour of several months, she is a former Tory agent in Brixton, Clapham and South London generally.

This has not been historic Conservative territory. (It is not for some people altogether London either.) Think of a midlands City set down on the far side of the Thames, is one judgment. Nor is the part nearer the river historically prosperous; some of the strongest roots were thrown down here by Labour in the days when Herbert Morrison was running the old London County Council. And not too much is remembered by Miss Lucas about her local Tories in the mid sixties with esteem. 'There were a lot of old and doddery ones and some very nasty ones. But you made do as best you could with the younger and nicer people.' She reckons that John Major knew her before she knew him. 'If he says he was sixteen when he first met me he'll be right, but I recollect him at twenty-three. But I'm afraid that before that time he would have been one of a good many youngsters I knew slightly.

'When I got to know him properly I had just formed North Lambeth Association, made up of Clapham, Brixton and Vauxhall. I was working with a couple of trainees.' (One suspects that in such unrewarding territory the agent willing to trouble herself will have exercised more than ordinary discretion and influence.) 'I used to take this young chap back from meetings in my car. He didn't have one and he would sit in the car for ages afterwards talking politics – we ranged over everything. In those days he lived at 24 Primrose Court. He had no furniture, only a chair and a carpet, a kettle and a record player. Though I don't know whether he was listening to Opera in those days, it may have come later with Norma.

'Of course he wouldn't get out of the car; he wanted to talk and we ranged over the whole political gamut, but we would go up occasionally and he would offer me the chair. One of his questions was, "Is there any future for somebody like me in the Conservative Party?" So I said, "Yes." ' Miss Lucas added delicately at this point that the week after our interview she would be taking up the same man's invitation to Chequers.

If slightly optimistic, she had given just about the right answer at that time. Heath the carpenter's son had just (1965) reached the leadership via Balliol and a commission; the driving force in the party was the odd alliance of Heath and Iain Macleod (claimed as a mentor by both John Major and Norman Tebbit who knew him quite well). Macleod, son of a Highland doctor, had nothing much to do with privilege or the social pyramid. (Neither, as he made his first incursion at this time, had Tebbit, son of Len the cyclist.)

But in 1967 a non-graduate with no prospect of a fortune rushing around in perpetual opposition politics in stonebound Labour South London was hardly a strong prospect for even a meagre parliamentary career with the Conservatives. However, History, as the Marxists might have said, would be on his side. So Miss Lucas got it right but not without optimism.

She told him a few essential rules for a career. For a start he needed some money, not necessarily the means of a wealthy man, but he must expect to spend upwards of five hundred pounds a year on contributions, fund-raising events and the like. (Even at 1968 prices this also sounds sanguine.) He must assemble a CV, perhaps on reflection he had that already – he had been Deputy Chairman, briefly Chairman of an Association and he was now a local councillor. That was enough to apply to be on the list of parliamentary candidates, but as he was young, it didn't absolutely follow that he would get on straight away after his interview with the candidates' vice chairman. He would in fact be put on that list, helped by an enthusiastic covering letter from Miss Lucas, but probably on the strength of his membership of a council.

That councillorship was a fluke, a fluke rewarding dedicated hard work, but like many things in politics, not in the hands of the subject. He had been made candidate at twenty-four for Ferndale Ward. Most wards in Lambeth were strongly Labour, Ferndale was notably so. In any other year most Tory candidacies would have been a pro forma affair, a mere going through the motions, however diligent the candidate. And indeed four years earlier in 1964 the twenty-year-old Major had submitted papers to permit the twenty-one-year-old Major to stand.

But this was 1968, Labour had just devalued the pound, Harold Wilson's honest, truthful, clubfootedly inept remark about 'the pound in your pocket retaining it's value' had been met with universal derision. Labour at or about this time were to lose three parliamentary seats, Meriden and Dudley in the West Midlands and Walthamstow West in East London (and once Clem Attlee's seat) by colossal swings. These are still recalled with affection, along with the 1962 Tory calamity of Orpington, as benchmarks of statistical atrocity.

That year in the London Borough of Lambeth, the Conservatives, makeweights almost constitutionally bound to opposition, won not just a victory but a near whitewash. Out of sixty seats Labour had three, the Tories fifty-seven. The balance before the election had been Labour forty-two, Conservatives eighteen. As the Labour agent heartbrokenly put it to Jean Lucas, 'We've lost everything.' The victory, one of those captivating things which happens to trainee politicians only as freak treat, almost led to the arrest of our Prime Minister. A friend of his, an older activist woman, had not had tickets for the count and had gone home to bed. 'We must tell Rose,' said the winner of Ferndale.

To this end he was apprehended by a policeman at one in the morning, three quarters of the way up a lamppost throwing handfuls of gravel at a window. What was all this then? Hadn't he heard? 'We've just won the council for the Tories and I'm the winner in Ferndale.' 'A Tory in Ferndale, that's impossible. I never heard of such a thing. You just get right down this minute, Sir. I must ask you to give an account of yourself.'

The thought occurs that if John Major states that he hates inflation and has seemed less impressible than many other Conservatives by the possibility of devaluation this year as a rational way out of Britain's problems, especially when faced with low competitiveness, that evening's result may have contributed to his state of mind and political mindset.

In fairness that wasn't the only influence upon this peculiar election. It was perfectly timed for maximum advantage to be taken of Mr Enoch Powell's 'Rivers of Blood' speech. Mr Powell, easing himself of an emotional imperative on the question of the coming race war caused by the arrival of Indian and Pakistani shopkeepers in large numbers, proclaimed doom, and was fired where he stood by his enemy Edward Heath. A point of view suddenly acquired a name, and a focus while a thousand nadgering debates were launched. The meat porters of Smithfield marched upon Westminster to proclaim their solidarity with Mr Powell. In Brixton where a large population of West Indian origin was firmly established, voters would take no notice of Mr Powell's subsequent remarks about the blameless irrelevance of black people from islands. They had heard immigrants denounced by a Conservative and none of the best intentions of Conservatives, from Mr Heath to the would-be-Councillor Major, could stop them winning votes by it.

A colleague at this time, a friend ever since, and now a colleague again, was George Young, already Sir George. The baronet is the archetypal liberal Tory, heavily involved in practical social policies and today Major's excellent choice for Housing Minister. He speaks with especial esteem for Bernard Perkins who after that election was quickly made leader of the Tory group, a pre-echo of the post-election coup of Ken Livingstone on the GLC, 'a major influence on me and I'm sure on John.' He points out that Perkins gathered a good deal of edge and command from his double life as a council officer as well as politician – he was deputy director of housing in Wandsworth.

Sir George recalls that the council was one of the first to turn against high-rise building and wholesale demolition of renewable housing. It actually called a halt to demolition work slightly ahead of the field. He also tells an amusing tale of confrontation with the unions. Recollections of most Conservative fights with the unions at about this time or a little later in Mr Heath's era are mostly of bad logistics, inadequate coal stocks and defeat. In the small world of Lambeth things went much better. The council was to be tested by the collectors of refuse. Habits of extreme overmanning had grown up over the years in municipal services. Treated by Labour administrations initially as a utility, then as a Tammany form of voter-protection and at all times as patronage for 'our people', the paytails of local government, known as direct labour, were a scandal and after fifteen years of Thatcher, and despite some efforts at sub-contracting, are not altogether erradicated. The habits of over-manning, low productivity and putting a moratorium on economics bite deep.

Beyond diseconomy and engaged in simple corruption were the South London dustmen, masters of their own institutionalized crimi-nality. Not getting their own way, the dustmen would strike on the happy assumption that a couple of weeks of black plastic sacks blowing along the streets while their spilled contents stank to heaven, would usually induce understanding and a spirit of accom-modation.

The Lambeth Tory leadership was liberal and good hearted but not feeble. They proposed that the ancient right of totting should be ended. Totting involved rummaging through the garbage for all things saleable, and splitting the proceeds (the dustmen at this time in South London kept receptacles like mini skips on their vehicles to stow the tottable). And as takers-away of furniture, metal and the odd antique, the dustmen were not fighting for rights to cabbage stalks. In fact totting had largely gone from other boroughs but Lambeth cherished its traditions.

The dustmen reacted to this uncalled-for reformism with the weapon of best resort, the strike. The council determined to stand and fight. We were coming into the 'Who governs Britain?' era, with exasperated though essentially moderate Tories asking the public to give them its general backing. For reasons that do not concern us here, that demand failed in the main forum, the February 1974 election, though with defter handling it wasn't doomed to. When the Tory council in Lambeth took on the ancestral pillage of the garbagistes, it did rather well.

As refuse collectors abandoned their carts, councillors borrowed army vehicles, the equivalent of those amateur fire engines, the green goddesses, and drove them around the streets of the borough. They were embarrassed with offers of large currency notes pressed upon them by shopkeepers accustomed to doing this to the regular street cleaners, often under the impression that it was a regular and legal charge. The explanation by councillors that all removal charges were covered by rates and government support payments and were performed quite free with no extras necessary by way of protection payments, came as a pleasant surprise. The quality of urban graft has quite a flavour.

Eventually, to their own surprise, the elected representatives found that in the man's world of loading bins on to trucks they could cope rather well. The prospect of an embarrassing display of part-time therapy by bespectacled men from offices doing the job in less time and explaining as they went that no additional payments were called for, had remarkable effect. In a surprisingly short time the totters saw the virtue of a politic surrender and returned to work. Mr Heath had cause to eat his heart out. Sadly, John Major was not able to drive a garbage truck for the good reason that he could not at this time drive at all. He would acquire a licence but only after his future wife, Norma, had remarked *on the way to the test* that he didn't know how to reverse round a corner, showed him and met him after his successful completion of the exam.

But though they were to perform surprisingly well, the Tories who came to power in Lambeth in 1968 had broken into a comfortable and well-established state of affairs. The old Labour leadership was strong at the top, had a handful of more or less competent people for key committees and was otherwise carrying dead weight.

A coming man also at the start of his career in this part of the world, watching council meetings from the public gallery, was Ken Livingstone. Red Ken is actually one of the more dispassionate judges of politics, rather better than most at avoiding the mists of partisanship. The Labour leadership in Lambeth, he says, was right wing, old fashioned and solid but entirely without imagination or ideas. Archie Cotton, the leader, and Jim Calder, his deputy, were 'competent and very reactionary in outlook. They instinctively looked at how far the rates could safely go up and would then build as many houses as that permitted,' a case of the means directing the ends. 'They were always scared of the ratepayers,' he adds. This has not been a feature of Labour local government in recent years.

But as Livingstone explains, a much earlier Lambeth Council had been badly bitten by dangerous originality. The young radical in those days had been Charlie Gibson of the T and G, later MP for Clapham, a man who incidentally had also made war on rackets, those run by his own unions on lines, as Ken puts it, of 'Look governor you haven't had a strike for a week.' Gibson's radical Labour group of 1919 had been advised by a sympathetic bank manager and had spent heavily on housing and come very badly unstuck in their only other council defeat. Like German inflation of the twenties, this had created a trauma and Archie Cotton, a man long in Lambeth Labour politics, had shared in the over-reaction.

But Livingstone is scathing both about the quality of Labour's council rank and file – 'some of them couldn't properly read and write, they were there to make up the vote' – and about the flavour of Labour politics. To the respectable if cautious Labourism of the Cotton leadership was added a good measure of simple racism. Take 'Black people and houses. The previous Labour Housing Chairman,' says Livingstone (actually he says 'chair'), 'was just awful. If he heard of a black family getting a flat he would go up the wall. So the Housing Director would just say quietly, "If you just give me that on paper, Sir, I will of course forward it to the lettings officer." So of course he didn't.'

This Housing Director is of the utmost importance in the career of John Major. His name was Harry Simpson. 'Some Housing Directors,' says Livingstone, 'are awful grey men concerned with catching up with arrears of rent. The atmosphere in Harry's office was more like a University.' This is a response echoed across the spectrum of every interview with anyone who had any acquaintance with Harry Simpson. 'I know what happened to John Major,' Livingstone adds, 'because it happened to me.' (In 1971 on Labour's resumption of power, the young Livingstone was made Vice-Chairman of Housing.) 'He took me round the worst areas where the overcrowding was, he took me to conferences, he was educating us.'

Simpson was very highly esteemed by national government. He would be asked by the Heath Cabinet to run housing in the province and work for Protestant-Catholic integration in Northern Ireland. That request came on the strength of his success with inter-racial housing in Lambeth. He would also go on to the GLC as Housing Director. Simpson, who died a couple of years ago, had direct effect, according to Ken Livingstone, on the people who mattered in the Lambeth Tory leadership. They had after all been elected on a fairly right-wing policy involving cuts in housing expenditure. 'He took Peter Carey (Deputy Leader of the Council) to see these places where there were six or seven Blacks sharing a room. And so he told me, Carey just said, "We were wrong," and went back and trebled the housing programme.'

'I don't know,' says Livingstone, 'whether Major was just another young reactionary when Simpson got hold of him or if he'd always been liberal. He did for him what he later did for me – "Go to this conference and that one," encouraging him to speak, as he encouraged me to speak, deluging us with books and papers so that we ended up mastering the brief we'd been given. He did all his manipulation quite openly, saying, "This is what I think you should do," not pretending to you that you'd thought of it yourself. So refreshingly, he told you the truth and educated you.' What did Simpson think of Major? 'He thought he was a brilliant man, he was going to go a long way.' Simpson's drift in Livingstone's twenty-year recalled paraphrase was: ' "He came in as a little right-winger who knew nothing and I educated him." But he thought the world of John and knew he would go far.'

Major himself has no doubts about the importance of Harry Simpson. 'I learned a lot from Harry. I would never deny that. He was the first person who showed me how bureaucracy can be used as a force for good rather than a force for interference.' He demonstrated to the young man 'how you could get to the other side of the table and help the people who were in need of help, rather than having them worry about the authoritarian aspects of the man in the suit and tie who sits opposite making the decisions.

'Simpson never,' says Major, 'exuded *that* even though he was a very powerful intellect.' Simpson in fact also left school early – at fourteen – to become an LCC rent collector. He had seen a great deal of the way people live ... and should not live.

'He had,' says his pupil, 'the great gift of bringing people into things instead of locking them out. He'd sit down before a meeting with a gin and tonic and explain what the questions were, what problems people had and what might be done to deal with them.' Simpson taught that 'you could achieve more by persuasion than by bludgeoning. A very valuable school to serve in, the Harry Simpson school of public service.

'He would take people who were totally opposed to his view, he would analyse their outlook, and the first thing he did was to understand their argument and why they made it. From that perspective you can dismantle it unless of course *you* get a better understanding and realize they may be right. If you operate from the other side of the wall without comprehending someone's thinking, you will never get through.

'With Harry Simpson, dealing perhaps with citizens distressed by some terrific grudge or wrong,' says Major, 'you saw him put himself inside other people's minds and watched him removing the gremlins. It was fascinating.' It is also immensely important to understanding John Major.

The period of office in Lambeth, during which he was on the Housing Committee from the start, was marked by setting up the advice centre and taking it on tour. He is proud of some houses built by the council for sale in the Myattsfield district for £8,000 each, and regretful about having accepted the general sixties delusion about high-rise building being a good idea. Some 'horrendous tower blocks were built,' though the old tenants and children were kept below the fifth floor on these properties.

Taking the advisory centre on tour, he thinks of as a wonderful experience. 'We would gather together the chairman and vice-chairman of Housing, the director, crucially, the lettings officer, and the director of planning and we would take them to face meetings of five, six, seven hundred people.' The numbers were so great because Lambeth was a housing stress area. He, Major, would open the meeting but then refer questioners to the official who had made the decision; for the first time the makers of decisions were answerable. Major was ardently keen and Harry Simpson also. 'Others,' he adds laconically, 'less so.' Interestingly, the experiment, which sounds like Periclean democracy brought to Lambeth, though enormously popular with the public, tenants of a stressed area, was one of those original and attractive ideas which somehow did *not* become general practice. With officials less enlightened than Harry Simpson, and politicians less instinctively responsive than John Major, one isn't in the least surprised.

In fact, as Livingstone acknowledges, there were other influences on the young man. The leader who had quickly emerged after a less than effective old timer, Charles Braxton, had been gently dropped, was Bernard Perkins. 'Bernard Perkins was a very liberal Tory and with Peter Carey as his deputy dominated things. Perkins was a council man. He had worked for ILEA as a school secretary, and became a clerk to governing authorities. He wasn't just a liberal Tory but incredibly bright and hard working.' There also was a chair of Housing, Leslie Aarons, 'nice and liberal,' says Livingstone, 'but very casual about working. So after a short while they dropped him and they had already worked out that Major was the brightest of the intake. There were about forty people elected who the leaders didn't know, except from going to occasional parties. Most of them were horrendously right wing, some of them had got themselves elected saying they would get rid of the Blacks.' (This is Ken Livingstone's political judgment and would be fiercely contested by Conservative witnesses of the group.)

Major then already had patrons in Perkins and Carey, to whom it was important not only that he was likeable and diligent, but that he rejected any hint of racism. He joined them as a member of the Housing Committee, then Vice Chairman and finally Chairman of Housing, running that expanded housing programme and establishing a system of constraints 'which was very strong giving all the powers to tackle bad landlords. They said,' reports Livingstone, ' "Here's the inspectors, here are the powers," and got them in there. And it did have a dramatic impact. It rapidly changed housing densities. They set up this housing advice centre in Brixton, very modern walk-in shop with comfortable seats where you'd come with all the problems that you'd got. It attracted national attention.'

The Labour Government, with Anthony Greenwood at the time as Housing Minister, issued a circular advising other councils to go and see what was being done and take it up. And during the election, the Tories had on their address, 'Mr Greenwood said this is the most imaginative housing policy in Britain.' 'The Labour Party,' he adds laconically, 'were pissed off. But it was quite justified. Given my views,' says Ken Livingstone, 'you just had to accept that in Lambeth the Tory Council, they were doing a bloody sight better than Labour and you had to acknowledge that as a benchmark before seeing what should be done to improve it.

'We didn't agree about them increasing the rents but they did introduce the most generous rebate system in Britain when many councils didn't have one at all. They occasionally did silly things like not giving free bus passes to the pensioners. But over all, they were very good. Most people in the Labour party became very fanatical because they were doing well. If they'd been fucking things up,' he remarks sweetly, 'people wouldn't have minded so much.'

Archie Cotton, incidentally, had been devastated by defeat; hair and teeth fell out and within a very few months he was dead. Having lived exclusively for politics he was wiped out by rejection. (One attempts earnestly at this point to resist later comparisons.) Otherwise the old Labour people who were left after the defeat in '68 – three members and five aldermen – 'they just got more frantically reactionary,' says Livingstone. 'You would sit in the gallery and hear them complaining about too many homeless families being looked after and Major answering that with needs the way they were, these places were just going to be built. You could have transposed the parties.'

Livingstone is not however too impressed by the Major claim (on his parliamentary candidate's CV) to have been involved in the sale of council houses. 'This was something they talked about in those days, the pre-Thatcherite macho line. "How many council houses did you sell?" I think I know how many they *did* sell: abut thirty-five. Basically, they must have decided it was a barmy idea and given up.'

The tone was prophetic too. 'If you listened to his second question time as Prime Minister when he started this stuff about, "How are we today?" and "Let's be reasonable," that was straight back twenty years. That was exactly how he handled things in Lambeth. His whole pattern was to defuse a political controversy if at all possible. I wasn't close. I wasn't a friend of his, he just struck me as someone who was very bright, incredibly hard working, incredibly loyal to Carey and Perkins. I never saw him rock the boat, or push himself in any shape or form. Basically in politics getting publicity is legitimate. You bloody make sure you get your working share of it. Publicity came to him but he never seemed to court it or push for it.'

Livingstone follows his sincere admiration for Major with a small bombshell from a somewhat later date. He wasn't sure who the real John Major quite was. 'We were waiting for a cab just after he'd got the Chief Secretary's job so I just said, "How on earth do you put up with all this reactionary crap given what you were doing down in Lambeth?" And he said, "You remember me, Ken. I haven't changed. And one day I'll be able to do what I want.'

Up to then he had thought of Major in parliament as a functionary, someone influenced by very strong personalities: Perkins, Simpson, Margaret Thatcher, and doing a good job of carrying out their policies. After that conversation he was not at all sure and felt that the right-wingers who elected Major had, from their point of view, made a mistake.

It was very strange that someone never seen to push himself could get to the top of the British political system when the whole thing 'was based on rampant political ambition and fifty years of struggle to get to the top.' His only reservation lay in the question: was there, along with the niceness, the vision and the manic drive possessed by a Thatcher or a Heseltine or indeed a Kinnock? How do you stay at the top of an appalling thing like politics if you're not driven? I've not seen evidence of John being driven. I can't think of anybody who's been Prime Minister about whom I'd be less surprised if he just said, "I've done enough of that. I want to do something else." '

Peter Golds, Tory, wit, original and South London contemporary, later agent to Rhodes Boyson ironically in Brent North, counterpart to Ken Livingstone's Brent South, gives another account, different in inflection and full of extra detail, but not at all contradicting it. He also is a fan of Harry Simpson and thinks his influence incalculable, and he includes the fact that Simpson's wife stood godmother to the Majors' daughter and first child, Elizabeth. He adds chapter and verse on Simpson's tours of instruction among the areas of gross overcrowding. 'Certain estates,' he says, 'were under the old Labour administration designated as Black. There would be such overcrowding that functioning gas stoves stood in bathrooms. There was one man whom we met on the landing. "Where did he live?" "He lived there?" "Sorry, where was there?" "The landing!"'

Incidentally, as both witnesses observe, Simpson, though not a party man, was almost certainly a Labour voter. This is not a pattern of influence and friendship which Mrs Thatcher could have practised. Golds also shares Livingstone's admiration for Bernard Perkins, 'an enornmous talent'; and he adds that Perkins, subsequently a sufferer from multiple sclerosis, never had any driving ambition. He became a serious candidate for a parliamentary seat later won by someone else, in Norwood. But for no apparent reason (perhaps incipient illness) he gave it up.

Golds has early recollections of the young Tories of South London (Vauxhall was for Yuppies; Brixton, Major's base, was the Cinderella). He recalls activists in that area: Ian Gow, involved at Clapham, Peter Brown, now Major's agent in Huntingdon, Marian Standish (now dead) at one time agent in Clapham; and among the GLC victors of 1967, Geoffrey Pattie and Gerard Vaughan, both subsequently middle-rank ministers. His recollection of Major is that set against his own immediate contemporaries, he lacked their gaucheness and awe of great ones. 'If we were in the presence of a candidate the rest of us were in shock, John swept in and talked with him levelly and easily, he *wasn't* in awe. He knew he would make it.' He also observes of Major's first candidacy in 1964 (an unsuccessful bid for a seat on Lambeth council) that given the time lags Major (born 29.3.43) may not at the time of adoption and submission of candidacy actually have been of legal age!

'We ran the party,' he says, 'out of George Robey House, an old music hall building at 332 Brixton Rd,' the only property owned by the indigent minority Tories of Lambeth.

Golds also remarks on the racial element though he thinks Ken Livingstone exaggerates its importance as a force for young Major to fight against. Though emphatically he didn't like it. There had been a number of Tory candidates in tune with Enoch Powell's Rivers of Blood speech, made early during the local government campaign. Three of them, Norman Epps, Alan Grey and David Renwick, standing together for the same ward, had put out an instant leaflet saying, 'We back Enoch. Don't you?' They were to be reprimanded. Renwick, though not notably involved in politics, subsequently forged for himself a big career in the news agency business, emerging as head of Reuters in New York.

Golds recollects other unengaging elements, a man called Bernard Black who did fight the Norwood parliamentary seat and made the issue of immigration and its evils his chief pre-occupation. There was a more direct involvement for Major in the person of James Harkes, parliamentary candidate for the 1970 election in Brixton. Harkes, according to Golds, was a virulent admirer of South Africa as it then was, a frequent visitor to that country and, together with his wife, acutely disagreeable.

She was to insult the sitting Labour MP Marcus Lipton, a courtly, decent elder figure very well liked by civil Tories. When Lipton offered his hand on the Town Hall steps, she refused it saying that she had only come to help her husband crush him. There were, according to other reports, lifelong Tories present at that incident who then entered the booths and voted Labour for the first time in their lives. Another observation – from Harkes himself – was, 'Heath's not normal,' something later disagreeably echoed by Mrs Thatcher to her liegeman, Sir John Junor. A *putsch* was planned against Harkes with Major very heavily involved. A neighbouring councillor, Diana Geddes (for whom as it happens a Miss Norma Johnson made dresses), was his nominee for the seat. The votes and the logistics were all ready and capable of delivery but the election was called with very little notice and the Tories were for the time being stuck with Harkes.

More generally, George Young has a cool and unalarmed re-collection of something which only attracted a distinct minority on the Tory side. 'There was a debate about it. John at once and very clearly identified himself with the moderate majority.'

The fullest account of the great race row is however given by Clive Jones. Jones, a genial man, originally from North Staffs who was a member of the 1968 Tory council and now doing solidly in the road haulage business, insists that we are talking about *two* distinct sets of people. The first part he says was the pamphlet put out by Renwick, Epps and Grey. They were fighting the most impossible seat of all, Bishops Ward, and would win only by double figures. Their line of being 'with Enoch, are you?' produced a variety of reactions, from appreciation that in a very adverse seat it was effective politics, to violent disapproval of the implied racialism. But nobody was punished for it, nor so far as he knows, reprimanded, certainly not expelled.

The second episode a few months later with the council *in situ*, concerns a letter drawn up by David Renwick which said that Lambeth had enough people there already and didn't want more coming in. As Jones recollects, fifteen people signed it though obvious liberals like George Young, Lawrence Kennedy and John Major were not approached for endorsement. He himself signed it, but saw it more as a parochial grumble aimed at general over-crowding and non-Lambeth incomers rather than specifically against Blacks. 'We were,' he says, 'naive and taken in by a couple of people who then manipulated the statement through the press.' In his view there was a hard core of real extremists. 'Alan Grey,' he says, 'despite his early signature, was nowhere near as right wing as the others.'

This letter was the subject of a formal telling off for the fifteen from Bernard Perkins in his office very much, he says, 'along the lines of, "Don't be bloody silly."' This disciplinary action was the exclusive concern, he adds, of Perkins, his deputy Carey and the whip, Hilary Jelly later Mrs Carey. John Major, though known not to care for such sentiments, was in no way involved in the reproof, he had no *locus standi* to do so. This is accurate though it misses Major's private exertions to which we shall come.

Jones himself, at that time parliamentary candidate for Vauxhall, has paid a very high price for a single appearance on a sheet of paper. Subsequently selected for Newham North East, his candidature was barred by Central Office almost certainly on the strength of that signature. This was the time of Mr Heath's 'purge of extremists', a well meant but slightly priggish and highly unscientific weeding which peremptorily designated as weeds all sorts of quite innoffen-sive plants.

On the race issue, which can be very confusing to the researcher, Major's own account of what happened finally clarifies matters. When David Renwick, Norman Epps and the slightly less culpable Alan Grey made their 'We back Enoch' statement, Major was too junior to be in any position to sack anyone or even give a reprimand. But he is very clear, not only about what he thought – total opposition – but is convinced that he took a leading role, talking to the Conservative leader, Bernard Perkins, in persuading him that this statement was not tolerable. He wasn't yet in a position to exact the discipline, but he spoke openly on the matter and had some fierce arguments on the question, making his own position very clear.

He was, as he would learn later, already thought of by Perkins as a prospective future committee chairman. Perkins was in fact already seeking him out for private discussions on policy. So he was listened to as he made his views clear privately and publicly. The official Tory condemnation did derive from Major's urgings and Ken Livingstone's recollections are, at least morally, correct.

The picture Peter Golds gives of party life as Major knew it in South London is full of contrasts, on the one hand influences for enormous good, the intelligent, humane, practical men like Perkins and Simpson, also the respected Peter Carey now dead. They reflected the best sort of minimally partisan politics, were pre-occupied with problem-solving, had a social purpose and could learn (Peter Carey's response on seeing the slums – 'we were wrong'). On the other hand there was also a disagreeable and genuinely racist faction, quite small in the view of both Young and Jones, seen in rather more vivid terms by Ken Livingstone, an honest witness but farther off. In between there seem to have been plenty of agreeable decent people like Clive Jones, right-of-centre Tories with old-fashioned reflexes, given to the odd unwise mutter into their beer, but not ill-disposed or deserving to be called racist.

Jones, who was a member of the Housing Committee for the second and third year was perhaps Major's closest friend at the time, certainly he was best man at his wedding. He tells of a social life which involved coming out of an earnest council or committee meeting, going for a beer at the pub opposite and then proceeding to a favourite takeaway. 'I had the car, John had more accessible accommodation so I would drive, he would lay on coffee in his room and we would share a single takeaway.' Before this suggests heart-rending notions of youthful poverty and the first act of *La Boheme*, he explains that the Brixton Road Indian place went in for such generous helpings that they needed no more. 'We would,' he adds, 'then settle down to put the world to rights.' Clive Jones also tells a couple of anecdotes, one of which has a distinct whiff of the

Childhood of Stalin, but echoes the later insistence of Huntingdon helpers about a quietly diligent if cheerful young politician.

'We were going one night along a road past the local cinema when suddenly John wasn't with me anymore. I turned back and he was on the ground, his leg, as it occasionally did, had failed him. The commissionaire of the cinema rushed up, a little crowd formed and we were going to drive him to hospital. He sits up and says, "No I'm supposed to be at the Tenants Association meeting, they're expecting me." We couldn't persuade him against going, so we got him there and I and the Tenants Association Chairman, who'd been phoned, pretty much carry him indoors. He does his meeting. And only then will he let us drive him to hospital.'

The second anecdote, lighter hearted and a conscious publicity move, concerns a Housing Estates meeting which was called for the morning of the Major wedding. They would have been happy to postpone it. But, for a lark and a little innocent publicity, Jones telephoned the *South London Press* and asked for a photographer for Saturday morning thus ensuring that a picture of Major and Jones in morning suits attending a housing estates meeting took the front page with the same (augmented) cast on an inside page for the wedding.

This is perhaps as good a place as any to introduce Major's future wife, Norma Johnson. During the 1970 GLC elections Norma was working for Diana Geddes the candidate, as well as being her dressmaker. She wanted to see the count but Mrs Geddes was out of passes so Norma was smuggled in as the girlfriend of Clive Jones (she wasn't).

The words of John Major to Peter Golds, there as an agent, were, 'Who is that pretty girl?' It was, says Golds, happy as matchmaker, chemistry at first sight. This was April, local government election time, by Summer they were engaged and in October 1970 they were married at Saint Matthew's Church, Brixton. The soprano June Bronhill, who had become a friend of Norma's on the circuit of the operatic mafia, sang at the wedding.

Peter Golds speaks admiringly of Norma Major, deriding any suggestion of unsophistication or mousiness. The opera was a total preoccupation for her, she was capable of loading her friends into a mini and driving them to Hamburg to see Sutherland. (This is a man speaking who to his eternal credit, takes ten days in New York in early January to see eight operas at the Met!) Incidentally, he assures us that the first opera to which she took John was Bellini's *Norma*. This is not someone to be taken lightly.

Clive Jones puts it succinctly: 'We were all in love with Norma. She was lovely.' 'Lovely in what way?' he was asked. 'Well you could take her for quiet some of the time and she was very gentle, but give her a subject she cared about like her opera and she'd become sparkling and bubbly.'

When the council term finally ended as it had to in Conservative defeat – 1971 being, in Ken Livingstone's phrase, 'the absolute pits of Heath' – the Lambeth Tories threw a wake/party at the Oval, a place close to the heart of their Chairman of Housing, and, politically speaking, retreated in good order. John Major had gained a wife and lost an office. The search for a life as full politically as personally now began.

3

Norma

Highest among John Major's good fortunes must be ranked his wife. The woman he had married after meeting at the Clapham committee rooms *en route* for the count at a GLC election in 1970 is a calm, unconfected person without a notion of grandness, distance or a desire to score. She will end by driving the fribble end of the press, social columnists and the like, to silent screams within their smart, well-appointed void.

Norma Elizabeth Christina Johnson (originally Wagstaff but her mother reverted to her maiden name after being widowed), was born in Much Wenlock but is not, as she points out, a Shropshire girl. The family came from London and her father, an Argyll and Sutherland Highlander, for wartime purposes was posted to the area. She also was brought up in South London, Peckham, another area which safely returns Labour MPs, though there was a later move to Beckenham where she would live again for a while after her marriage. Her father in civilian life worked at the less exalted end of the print trade and had some talent as a pianist. There was no money for he died early but she acquired good enough schooling at Peckham Comprehensive to go on at eighteen to teacher training, specializing in Domestic Science with a strong line in dressmaking (her grandmother had worked in men's tailoring). For five years she taught this subject at St Michael and All Angels Church of England School, Camberwell.

She liked that work very well. But wanting a temporary break and pursuing her passion for opera and the theatrical world generally, she struck up a very good relationship with the operatic soprano June Bronhill and took a short-term job with her, making clothes, driving, and generally being of use. But she was also building up a steady little business as a dressmaker, Diana Geddes, the GLC client, whose count she wanted to watch on the historic night, being one of her clients. They had also met through Peter Golds. Because of Diana's candidacy she went to the count and on the way there at the committee rooms, on 3 April 1970, was introduced to this chap.

'What about him? Well what can one say? He seemed quite a nice chap, bit pushy, bit bossy, inclined to throw his weight around a bit – in the nicest possible way. I just thought he was nice and rather good company. I was also rather impressed that he was on the council. Also councillors got invited to quite nice things.' She was not certain of the Peter Golds legend of taking John to Bellini's *Norma*. She thinks the first occasion was a gala for Sir David Webster. She was a pavement queuer and would go in a group, everyone buying his own ticket. John was rather annoyed the first time that she didn't have one for him. 'Sorry but I didn't know you when I got this one.'

She had been pleased to hear of his going to a performance of *Elijah* but came to think of him as a Gilbert and Sullivan fan who could with care be induced to go to the real thing. She normally chose carefully for their outings, but once had to take him blind to *Die Meistersinger* ('Oh' he had said, perhaps ironically, 'I thought it was a folk group'), and found that he liked it, all five hours, better than any other. He was, she insists, to be more generous than she in one respect – 'I haven't been to a cricket match with him yet. It does go on all day doesn't it?'

The marriage, to accelerate a fast moving episode, took place on 3 October, not long after the death of his mother whom she was to meet only a very few times. They lived for the interim in a flat in Streatham before moving in 1973 to Beckenham. (Elizabeth, their first child, was born within a week of his selection in 1971 for St Pancras North.) With its paddock and wood, the West Oak Estate, Beckenham, was more rural than the future home in Huntingdon. She had not fully realized everything, in terms of work, grandeur and loss of privacy, that marrying a political aspirant involved. But she has particularly happy memories of the West Oak days. He was seeking a seat, toying with the idea of Bromley Council and being put off it by her, since she knew what he really wanted.

He was busy enough then but not in the all-pre-empting way of very recent years. He was not incidentally, in his wife's view, actually so very happy with the bank but they could live pleasantly trying to make the political career happen. She recalls the pleasure of being in on many Saturday and all Sunday nights for the ritual of having supper off trays while watching *The Onedin Line*. 'It seems an age ago, we never do things like that now,' she says. He was capable enough about the house. Her mother would ask if he wanted to make the meal or bath the children and he would comply, but on the other hand, he had neither taste not aptitude for gardening.

Even the politics at this time was more larky than it has become. There was the frantic call when he had to go for his interview for the Candidates' List at Central Office. The zip had gone in his trousers, could she bring the spare pair? – even the famous one suit has its resources. She did and he changed in the car. Another example of enjoyment, she had been swept along in St Pancras by the warmth and optimism of supporters into thinking against all judgment that he might win, though she notes that if he had, it would have been a disaster for his career.

She observes in him one quality not evident in Mrs Thatcher. On a recent Spanish holiday he had managed, apart from the occasional call to the office, not to do a stroke of work, in marked contrast to an earlier Spanish trip and a non-stop study session at the Villa Jones as a new Foreign Minister. It might not work longer than a fortnight but he could switch off.

Back with the political ascent, Huntingdon had come as a mild surprise to her. 'He looked at the post in bed one Saturday,' she recalls, and said, "Oh, I've got an interview for Huntingdon". This was at a time when after finishing with St Pancras North in October 1974 and having made no progress in a succession of seats, Ruislip, Paddington, Portsmouth and Dorset South, he was somewhat despondent, given to saying, 'This is the last one,' not that it ever would have been. She didn't even know he had put in for this one but she was pleased, since they had friends nearby and had spent holidays at neighbouring Bourn. She thinks of Huntingdon as 'a fabulous constituency which we were very lucky to have.' Today her friends and activities are there. Though there are one or two girlfriends among ministerial wives: Caroline Ryder, Alison Wakeham and Judy Hurd – all nice, none dashing – are mentioned.

She recalls that a friendly member of the Huntingdon association, Ann Ford, took out a bet that John would become Chancellor before 1990! However, though she seems to have walked little scathed through the snobbish resentments, of which their friends and supporters were sharply aware among the County element, she did sense that there were groups to whom they only became accept-able *because* John was a prospective MP. She does not, in the sitting room of the Downing Street flat, glory in the fact. She is more than a little amazed and well aware that in some circles yet, they would both be 'little people' to be disregarded but for the unanswerable grandeur of accomplished rank. Although feelings like that occurred and although John had his bouts of despondency on the way up, especially when making slow progress towards a seat, she scouts the newspaper story that he had contemplated going to America. If he had ever thought of it, it would have met with her wholehearted resistance.

But when the break came, most of Huntingdon, ordinary Hun-tingdon, had been very kind and welcoming at once; she speaks of a friendly area. On 8 December 1977 after a typical delay over accomplishing the move, they shifted to a house in Hemmingford Grey within the constituency, they would later move to their present house, 'Finings' in Great Stukeley.

As a candidate at the count she recalls his extreme anxiety, 'I'll lose, I'll lose.' Sir David Renton and his wife could not have been kinder, but their majority was a touch albatross-like, could he live up to it? (In fact he doubled it.) She had been affected by this and by kindly meaning county types saying, over and over again, 'Of course you realize you can't hope to do as well as David.' Everything in recent years had been hard for them, house moves very slow and hitting every wrong angle thrown up by gazumping. All this had induced pessimism. 'So the effect is that you begin to think, "Here is this lovely constituency and, my God, we're going to lose it,"' proof surely of wanting something very much.

Once he was elected she had not, by reason of the children, been a great gallery flower or parliament follower, she had not heard his maiden speech nor, in February when we spoke, heard one of his question times, but readily watched the televised version. One day in 1983 he rang up and asked her if he should take up the offer of a job in the Whips' Office. He had of course been aching for advancement for the previous four years, and the early promotions of the Pattens and others, of a parliamentary career which actually began rather slowly. But there were financial penalties. He had to give up the income from the bank's advisory post which he had taken on becoming a Member, and their preferential mortgage took a knock. But she had never tried to hold up any part of his political career.

In fact, she has a nice nostalgia for these days in the Whips' Office. When he came back for the weekend, (the pattern of out-of-London MPs' lives), he did not have red boxes. He would have a bath, she would make him a cup of tea, come and sit on the lid of the loo and, without betraying earnest secrets, John, being a very good raconteur, would tell her all the funny things and have her laughing. He is, she says, someone who can be enormous fun to be with but, to be honest, in the last couple of years she has missed that.

Their two children, Elizabeth born 1971 and James born 1975, have been the business of her last two decades, though she feels alternately guilty according to whether she is in London not seeing them or in Huntingdon not being near John. The previous week she said, James's housemaster at Kimbolton School asked him, 'How often is your mother at home?' There is more pressure on her but the routine hasn't changed. Elizabeth, now training to be a veterinarian, 'has a lot of John in her': decisive, fast thinking, knowing what she wants to do. James is 'more laid back', easier-going, could try harder, thinks of accountancy, having some head for maths, but anyway is calm and relaxed.

Elizabeth has been known to grumble about the great paternal career, has been sardonic – 'If he becomes Prime Minister, I'll shoot myself.' But when they did come to discuss the looming possibility, her actual reaction was, 'Go for it, Dad.' She would appear to be the one person upon whom the Major genius for getting people nicely to do what he wants, wholly fails to work. Norma speaks of 'the only times sparks ever fly in our house' being in arguments between father and a daughter quite significantly like him. Norma had known that his whole line of argument over Elizabeth's choice of career was calculated to be counter-productive so why couldn't he stop or change tack? But such conversations had a way of ending with him exasperatedly saying, 'Oh, it's useless trying to talk to you,' after not getting through, something which would astound any number of cabinet colleagues. Though in fact he does see the makings of political talent in her.

Norma's own feeling about her husband is that his real ambition had been, quite genuinely, to be Chancellor, but saying, as we all do, that she doesn't believe in horoscopes, she remembers reading in the summer of 1990 predictions for both their configurations and being told in both of a very big upheaval and advancement and thinking, 'God, surely not Prime Minister.' She feels guilty about wanting to see more of him when the work is so hard and the crises keep coming but then, as she says, she doesn't want much. And she does observe the effect upon John of hard, driven work. She observes that he is very good company, something any observer will vouch for, but there is inevitably an element of theatre about this and he is not, as he used to be, such fun when the public action is over. Having put himself out, he is more likely in private simply to slump. This was however said at the height of the war and all the weariness that it brought. Her basic message remained that looking like a nice chap, he actually was a nice chap.

It may be apt, having seen Norma through her own eyes, and something of John through them, to invoke the opinion of a friend well placed to make a judgment. Emily Blatch, a family friend from 1976 on (in Cambridgeshire) and now a minister in the Lords, speaks of Norma's passion for Joan Sutherland, the time in the gods, the research, the thousands of miles of travel to Australia and wherever in pursuit of her book on the soprano, none of which speaks the spiteful newspaper talk about dimness and dowdiness.

Norma's enthusiasm for opera would eventually produce a book, a life of Joan Sutherland. Longstanding dedication to the cheerful Australian soprano would produce in a supposedly shy person the nerve to make her acquaintance. The friendship with June Bronhill fostered this confidence, and having won Sutherland's trust and that of her husband, Richard Bonynge, she would begin a bibliography of the diva, a bibliography which would turn across ten years into a biography. It was to be solidly and gratefully reviewed though it was a work achieved against the grain of Norma's untheatrical personality. Much talk of a second book, a life of Jessie Norman, is unfounded. No such book was or is planned, though offers and proposals have been bandied about. On the strength of what she has done it would give great pleasure if she should turn herself to another such study.

She is, incidentally according to Lady Blatch, the practical one, the one who knocks the nails in, who being rather strong, actually works the rods on the septic tank which serves the house at Great Stukeley. 'He's not hot at that, John, not too hot,' she adds sweetly. But also, she says, Norma is a shy and private person. She has enormous commitment to Elizabeth and James. They have reached what for any child is the difficult time, the late teens, era of exams and just getting through school. Perhaps, she speculates, James might personally choose to go for his sixth form stretch to a boarding school but in no way will she pack him off.

In her view Mrs Major would give the lie to the sneering talk by demonstrating the considerable if understated elegance of which she was capable when the time came for Downing Street hostessing. But she was primarily a worker. Her role in charity in the constituency which concerned Mencap and latterly Rumanian children, had always involved *doing* things. 'She never wanted to be merely on the letterhead as "Mrs Norma Major, Patron."' Involvement in Mencap derived from a commitment by John's predecessor, David Renton.

But to raise funds Norma actually completed a marathon in 1990, walking rather than running, but who is insisting? That effort had been worth £5,000 to the organization. 'She flogs the christmas cards and gifts at Christmas,' says Lady Blatch. 'She runs a fund-raising quiz in the constituency with all the branches entering teams to work up to the final. She assembles the questions, organizes the timetable, running the final itself direct. It raises enormous amounts.' The question of the Rumanian babies had moved Norma Major very much. 'I just feel I've got to do something,' had been her reaction, so she used her musical connections to organize a concert in St Ives.

She was also an active worker in local politics. If a group of people were fighting a county council she would give each of them a day in support in different parts of the constituency. This of course is extremely useful to the MP since it keeps a network of contacts in very healthy order. 'If you have a day with Norma, you quickly see she *is* known there.'

'If somebody was ill in the constituency it isn't unusual to hear that Norma had been to the hospital,' says Lady Blatch, 'but it would never be publicized. She would never want exploitation of kindnesses.' This is kin with another aspect of Mrs Major, the private person, cool about publicity, who practises with very old friends the almost defunct art of long-letter writing. Old friendships evidently matter.

They matter this much. On the night of the first ballot when the heavens were falling, Emily Blatch, asked round to Downing Street, slipped out of the reception and found Norma in the kitchen consoling a friend on the phone. Because of the sudden market in the Majors, the friend had been rung up by a reporter asking first for her husband. The husband had in fact been dead for a very few weeks and the friend had collapsed into tears. Norma was concerned in the middle of all the great events that the friend should be gently reassured, helped to realize that it was an unlucky mistake and simply be cushioned from hurt.

She also reacted with a different sort of compassion to the chief loser of the St Cecilia's Day Massacre, Margaret Thatcher. She was fond of that lady, feeling her much maligned, 'a much nicer person inside the distant clinical public person,' as Emily Blatch puts it. 'What I want to do,' said Norma, just after the Thatcher resignation on 22 November, 'is to throw my arms round her. I want to express a warmth to her.' In fact she did do just this and was able to say, 'I *have* put my arms round her.'

As for family, Emily Blatch describes children of extravagant normality: James, footballer and general sports enthusiast accustomed to cricket, football and cinema excursions with his father whenever possible; and Elizabeth, now training to be a vet, also 'a very competent clarinettist', able to hold her own in school concerts and scheduled to play at a concert at the neighbouring US base.

Emily Blatch also describes the sort of jollification which will be growing ever rarer. 'John had reached the stage where the security grows tighter and the official car more obligatory. But there were guests, I think the Mellors, so they had this excursion to see *ET* or a film of that sort. The two families went to the new multi-screen place in Peterborough. It was difficult to do when you are Foreign Secretary – tremendous kerfuffle, all lined up in the foyer and the security man buying the tickets. It isn't the sort of thing they will be able to do now.'

Indeed not, Norma Major has since described an obnoxious man in a restaurant in February, when she had tried to go with her children and friends for a Greek meal, asking if she was Mrs Major because he didn't think she could be – where were her heavies? Three men stood up – anyway, what was she doing round there?' She also described Elizabeth's tight-lipped fury at the intrusion.

All of Norma Major's happiest recollections are of fun on the long journey up, and of private humour and companionship, also of innocent excursions. Available now is the cold glitz-face of official entertaining combined with a sort of ambulating siege wherever she goes. None of this will be caused by things she wanted for herself. Against it she can stack whatever privacy and friendship can be sustained in Huntingdon and also, if she wanted, the companionability of politics itself, not the worst of company. She remains a sane, soothing, self-evidently admirable member of the good middle of things, as a role model for decent people, a vast improvement on dumb royalty or the Chic. But that will be only partial consolation to her.

4

Waiting for the Call

During the period following defeat on the council, and the inevitable swing back to Labour in 1971, Major was hampered by the odd fact that he knew no Conservative MP to sponsor him for the Candidates List of which he had first spoken to Jean Lucas. His background of Young Conservatism had brought the odd member to speak and they had not awed him, but he lacked acquaintance strong enough to warrant this sort of political bank guarantee. Marcus Lipton was still his only friend in the Commons!

By chance he now spoke at a meeting at Kennington where Jill Knight, then as now the strong-minded, well-liked MP for Birmingham Edgbaston, was also on the platform. She was impressed and asked if he wanted to go into politics. He did indeed but explained his predicament. She expressed herself willing, but he, in the shy way of aspirants, wasn't sure if she really meant it. So he wrote to her and she made her willingness very clear. Accordingly, the form giving her name as a referee went away to Central Office. They would take an eternity to do anything about it. There is very little Albania can teach Conservative and Unionist Central Office about bureaucracy or Buddhism teach applicants about patience.

For Major this was to be a period of seeking a parliamentary career. He had a job at the bank. He was no longer seeking to go to Africa for long spells and not yet overseen by a patron. (Lord Barber, who would perform that role, was still struggling with Mr

Heath, Mr Scargill and the economy.) He was also making a home.

The Majors removed soon after the '71 defeat to Beckenham in Kent to West Oak Estate. David Rodgers, a neighbour at this time, who has remained in contact, describes it as a pleasant grouping of about fifteen houses round a shared wood and meadow. Major became quite soon involved in the residents' association. 'I don't think he was more than treasurer,' says Rodgers, 'but he effectively ran it, always trying to avoid conflict. There were differences of interest according to income and long-term intentions of residence and plenty of squabbles after he had gone, but he had a way of having a word with someone before a meeting to head off trouble. What you remember about, was all the trouble which didn't happen when he was there.'

In this community round its meadow there was no need for baby sitters from outside, Rodgers says. He recalls coming back from France with his wife, both utterly tired, and John Major taking over their children, serving up the now notorious Major baked beans on toast. Mr Rodgers, a highly political animal himself, makes the point that his own two children had remarked on a difference between the conversation of other MP friends visiting the house, who were preoccupied with the activity and ambitions of politics, and the conversation of John Major who talked about ideas and subjects, but *not* about the great game of politics.

But ambition was working in its quiet way. Rodgers also remembers picking up his Heather from ballet class at the same time as his neighbour was collecting his Elizabeth and recalls him jumping out of the car and saying excitedly, 'I've got it, I've got it.' He meant Huntingdon and membership of the Commons. That, however, lay five years ahead. He was in 1971 a former one-term councillor, treasurer of the residents' association, and had a middling job in a bank.

It was, despite a party branch chairmanship, a period of relative or apparent inactivity. David Rodgers remembers favourite pubs in the town, the Jolly Woodman and the George; he asserts the notorious Major weakness for Indian takeaways (denied by the Prime Minister) mentioning two in Beckenham where he was a fixture, and describes a pattern of unThatcherian conduct. 'There was a pub near Blackfriars station, the Old Blackfriars, where in the evening if we had missed the train we would go for a pint and if we felt like it would miss the next train.' One suspects that sentence may be worth hundreds of thousands of votes to Major. The thought of Mrs Thatcher ever travelling on a train, let alone missing one, still less going for a drink in the meanwhile, does not quite focus in the mind.

David Rodgers makes a nice point about one of those train journeys. 'The train stopped agreeably for us opposite a cricket match. We watched it in the evening sun. I watched the batsman look round the field and said, "He's looking for the fielders," "No," said John, "He's looking for the gaps."'

The chief political enthusiasm of Major's which Rodgers remembers – as a former worker for that politician – was Iain Macleod. 'He possessed, and often played, a record put out by Central Office, of Macleod's speeches. He was at this time also a firm advocate of comprehensive schooling, agreeing that children had unequal cultural opportunities for which comprehensives would be a corrective. This was a commonplace even among Conservatives at the time. The Black Papers against current educational trends were only just launched and the minister ironically engaged in killing off more grammar schools than ever in a single term was Margaret Thatcher. But whatever the charm of ideas Major still pursued serious, parliamentary, politics.'

It is doctrine among all aspiring candidates that you undergo ceremonial humiliation by fighting an unwinnable seat. Things came right at this hurdle according to Peter Golds after a short, intense bout of frustration. At Tory Party Conference in 1971 at Blackpool Major was determined to speak, a sensible aproach this, since Conference for the outsider aspiring to get in, is something of a show, not quite Miss World, not altogether Cruft's, but with the feeling of both. Not everyone can be Edwina Currie, whirling handcuffs round her head like a gaucho demonstrating the bolas. But a well-judged intelligent and/or fiery speech can ring the right bells with hard-eyed agents hanging around the place like so many football scouts.

It was Major's luck at this time that having prepared a speech for every important debate, a dozen or more, he had not at the end of the week been called for any of them, which given the favourable publicity won by Lambeth Housing Committee suggests doziness on the steering committee greater even than its admired norm. However, Peter Golds fell to talking with his friend, Tony Dey, agent for St Pancras North, a safe Labour seat and one already far advanced in the selection of a candidate. Major's beauties were described to Dey who, pleased with a progressive council record and all the local party offices, asked for formal application to be made at once. It was delivered by Major by hand with an hour to spare.

In the less frantic world of unwinnables he was interviewed, shortlisted and subsequently selected by Mr Dey's modest but trim little machine before Central Office got round to telling the now prospective candidate for St Pancras North that as an admitted member of the list he might like to apply for candidacies. Central Office carries Conservative belief in self-reliance a little far.

All this time Major had had a parallel life, work. He had of course been pursuing his job with the Standard Charter Bank. He had performed a variety of duties including the physically disastrous trip to Africa, he had worked briefly on the foreign exchange market, not yet the rodeo at which loads-a-money characters with sharp, ante-post Kempton Park arithmetic, could put together a quarter of a million a year before nervous collapse at thirty.

He had subsequently, however, graduated to what was effectively development banking, heavily concerned with Africa, occasionally going to places like Zambia but chiefly concerned to facilitate and promote investment in African countries through a series of companies, most of them in the infrastructure: road builders, civil engineers, builders of dry docks and the like. They were advising companies giving advice on trading opportunities in countries like Zimbabwe.

Much has been made of Major's role working direct to Anthony Barber, the former Chancellor (1970–4) who was chairman of the bank between 1974 and 1987. He was in fact personal assistant only for the period of the 1976 IMF conference in Manilla. This was the conference that should have been attended by the actual Chancellor, Denis Healey, compelled by the ferocious fall in the pound to have his car turn round at the airport. The considered view of people friendly to John Major at the bank is that while, obviously, he must have attracted some attention as a development hand and thus a suitable man for a conference where development finance would be centrally important, it is possible to overrate the importance of the appointment.

Will Manser, friend and colleague of Major, makes the point that Barber, as a former cabinet minister, was accustomed to having an aide, someone to lean on, companionship and a mark of status. It was creditable for Major to be chosen, but there is no evidence that at this stage Major had been spotted by his boss as an especially high flyer. A senior banker is rumoured to have conducted an inquest much more recently into how banking had managed to let such a talent slip through its fingers to take up a marginal career.

On the other hand he had broadly made a mark with superiors as a man worth promoting. His internal move, with Manser as deputy, to Corporate Affairs had come at about the same time as the Manilla trip. In the past, insists Manser, the status of Public Relations, for which Corporate Affairs is a fancy new word, had not been high in banks. It had been he said, the sort of job given to someone not thought to have been up to it in real banking. That absolutely and categorically had not been true of Major. He had been quite excellent at development finance. Manser describes him at work. 'There would be meetings when we were both in mainstream banking, where we would be totally outnumbered. And not only would he come out having won against those odds – and bankers by and large are a very grey bunch who get nasty when they lose – but there would be absolutely no animosity against him. Knowing that, though he was nobody in politics but had beliefs, I would feel "I really hope John does well in politics" but the experience would also tell me that I should never get involved in politics because I would never be that good.'

One of these encounters won by Major concerned the taking of a policy view within the bank about providing facilities in Africa. 'John thought that short- and even medium-term views were not relevant when a continent of enormous importance would be there in the long term. He argued very forcefully and effectively for keeping a presence and an interest.'

Something else Manser recalls is that either through natural ability or through a photographic memory process, he had an enormous talent for grasping a brief. He would pick it up, read and take it in immediately. That must, he feels, have been important when his colleague first went to the Treasury.

Manser stresses the extent of the economic geography in which Major immersed himself simply by doing the development job. 'There was a measure of travelling for John but at Standard Charter there was a regular flow through the office of our own people who had been in the field and who were regularly bringing us both up to date.' He is unimpressed by stories of Foreign Office mandarins alleged to have been cool and amused by Major on his arrival at the FO. (In fairness FCO people express horror at the stories.) 'Those reactions,' he remarks, 'would come from clockwork clerks who had been posted where they had been told to go, so that their knowledge of the world was on Foreign Office briefs and involved nothing outside the Embassy Compound.' Major's friend and long-serving colleague has a pungency when talking about élites which echoes very closely his own robust reaction to hierarchs and inheritors.

What was happening immediately though was a restructuring of Public Relations to make it work, precisely because the company wanted to educate the press and public in its own special different nature as a bank. Lord Barber had asked Major to take on PR to get it reorganized. It was no longer to be just a buffer between the management and the press, but to spell out and articulate what the Bank was about and in which ways it differed from the banking norm. 'He started the department up from almost nothing and made it his business to cultivate the city editors and best intelligences in the press for the Bank.' It was important to have it understood that essentially SCB was an international bank, the fifth largest of British banks, it was spread around fifty countries with 700 offices between them, of which only twenty were in the UK. Accordingly they were not exposed to the specific problems of UK banks.

Manser, warming to the task of Head of Corporate Affairs (he succeeded Major) went to work to sell SCB to me. They had always recruited entrepreneurial people who had character in the right or wrong ways. An SCB man might be 'an expatriate Scot weaned away from Glasgow at eighteen and spending his life in Hong Kong, someone different in character to a bureaucrat clinging to the safety of Stow in the Wold, whose career would come right if he was a good lad.' All of that, he added, appealed to John. 'The characters we have here, they are not conventional in City terms and John was right for this organization at the time he was here.'

The personal relationship had been very pleasant with no friction but Manser had been aware that Major was in charge, also that he needed to take less time on the briefing process than anyone around him. 'He would give credit to colleagues and very graciously, but you realized he was giving a good ninety per cent so you couldn't afford to slack off. In a meeting his political astuteness would always win the day even if we didn't deserve to.' So he could sell a duff bill of goods if he had to? 'Oh absolutely.'

He had not been there only on a pending basis, however keen the political ambitions. He had liked it there and been happy, especially with the international aspect of his work. I wondered aloud what might have happened if Major had *not* gone into politics? Manser was emphatic. In the city as it had developed lately 'with the old school tie deferring to the ability to sell and sell yourself, John would have done extraordinarily well. He would have been in the top calibre. He had a presence which mixed old and new, something which was extraordinary, and he had natural ability. If barrowboys could be earning £200,000 he would have been way above that and with a permanent position. He would now have had a directorship at the top level.'

What about politics, did he talk politics much or express strong opinions when with colleagues? 'He didn't do so much, but he did have very strong and passionate views on society and social equality. We could be scanning the City pages of a morning and John would come in and pull something from the front page and say, "God, how can people be allowed to live like this?" And he would have very, very clear views about it: poverty, housing and factories he was very close to.' So the socially conscious side of him was for real? 'Oh undoubtedly, oh yes.' Then apart from one or two things like the money supply, he was not really a Thatcherite at all? 'Oh I think that's right.'

He began to relate the colleague he had worked with to the here-and-now Prime Minister, noting the similarities, but also the political change he believed they would bring about. He thought there was going to be a big departure; circumstance would help bring it about. Witness the war situation. He was using his skills, spending a great deal of time talking to people. His communication with other political parties 'was better than we've had for a decade.' His communication with leaders overseas was better too: he was spending an immense amount of time actually talking to them and forming a view. Manser was impressed at the want of a reaction to the tricky behaviour of Francois Mitterrand in launching his peace initiative within hours of meeting the new British Prime Minister whom he did not tell about it. Major hadn't reacted. 'Could one imagine how Thatcher would have created and the first-class Anglo-French crisis that would have followed? For all that it had been hurtful to John at a time he needed to establish his credibility; that restraint was astuteness, a really astute reaction.'

By way of an afterthought he observed, looking to the future, that the harm done by war on the Third World through disruption of trade would be what would chiefly concern Major. Banking then was seen by this key colleague as a sphere where Major succeeded, but where large qualities to fit a bigger stage were perfectly evident. Manser had talked without surprise at his old boss's elevation.

But in the mid-seventies all political advancement for this bank servant was by small steps. In the midwinter of 1973–4 Edward Heath, then Prime Minister, made a number of important mistakes. Worsted by the National Union of Mineworkers once already in 1971, he had made no adequate provision of coal stocks, had believed rightly in the good will, wrongly in the ability to deliver, of the Union's national leadership. He had erected an elaborate pay policy and a yet more elaborate (and highly inflationary) exception for the miners to win that undeliverable promise and was reduced to spelling out the extent of his concession – $16\frac{1}{2}$ per cent as he entered the dispute. He then sought to turn the strike into an election but rejected the early date, 7 February, on which he would have won, for the 28th on which he would lose.

The delay created time for him to concede one of those arbitrations of surrender headed by a judge to which the electorate had grown derisively wise from the Wilson years onwards. Having been asked, 'Who rules?', an electorate which actually quite respected him, returned the perplexed answer, 'Well, not you for sure.' In these circumstances Major, two years after selection for St Pancras North, found himself committed on that February date a little ahead of customary schedule, to fight his statutory unwinnable seat. The future Prime Minister had also been given a classic chessplayer's example of a succession of passed pawns, open files and wild sacrifices. He had been shown how not to do the job.

Selection to fight St Pancras North back in 1971 had taken him as far as a South Londoner hopes to go in life, lower Highgate. This, together with Camden Town, Chalk Farm and Kentish Town, made up the constituency. Its key man in Major's own eyes was Bob Bell, 'a lovely man from Highgate who was everything to that association: organized the club, opened it, closed it, everything.' Another friend was Joan Cousins, 'pretty right wing, regarded me as reasonably able but dangerously civilized.'

He would write press releases which she would transcribe and type before, for the Hell of it, writing alternative press releases, 'absolutely outrageous ones, I mean absolutely outrageous,' saying the right-wing things she would have liked him to say. She was gifted as an artist and despite obvious political differences 'we got on amazingly well right from the start.' There were other friends and colleagues as Major remembers them: Mrs Brennan, Roland Walker, who was Treasurer for ages, Roland Klein and Martin Morton, also from Highgate, who had led Camden Council Tories. It wasn't a strong association but a tightly bound and enthusiastic one which worked the constituency very hard, treating it as a marginal 'which,' says Major, 'it was not.'

It was a safe Labour seat but the local Labour Party lacked the geniality associated with electoral ease. His agent, now that Tony Dey had moved to more rewarding territory, was Sue Winter, much newer to the seat and only twenty at the time. She recalls the insistent rudeness and aggression of Labour activists during the election and recalls that, against the normal earnest tenor of such proceedings, they were given to bringing half bottles of scotch into the count. Ms Winter, no Tory particularist, says that the rudeness and brutality of this constituency was not part of her experience of the Labour Party elsewhere. But this one had a bad reputation, very ready to be directly insulting to Tories. At twenty and just starting, she was frightened. The local Tories by contrast, were the nicest association she in eight years as an agent worked with, perhaps because they had no hope of winning.

The sitting member Jock Stallard was thought of, she says, as a very good constituency member. But for some reason he and the local Labour Party 'absolutely loathed John'. (Jock Stallard absolutely denies this.) But at a later date Major would tell Sue Winter that 'These days Jock Stallard comes and pumps my hand warmly, treats me like a long lost brother and we get on extremely well and funnily enough, we agree about almost everything.' (Jock Stallard denies that as well.)

Ms Winter thought of her candidate as terribly old. In 1974 he was exactly thirty. She also thought 'he was going to be very conservative and not very exciting to work with. After about half an hour of talking to him I realized I was absolutely wrong, that there was far more than met the eye.' He was, in fact, 'one of the funniest men I've ever met.'

As a working candidate, 'he could always handle street traders, didn't come over like a politician, was not pompous and was easy with people.' He had been irked though when the wall at the Leighton St headquarters of the Conservatives, which had just been whitewashed, received the message, 'Not a Major success.' She recalls sending him a card when he became Chancellor with the words, 'Well so much for "not a Major success".'

One minor success was to scare the incumbent. There was never a chance of winning, he says, but 'for a few days Jock Stallard was really worried.' There were a few enclaves of solid Tory support inside this essentially safe seat. So good organizing brought out that February a flush of bluebells by way of Tory Posters in concentrations which scarily overstated Conservative strength and gave Mr Stallard a brief flurry of anxiety before his own canvass came in. The Tory canvass itself Major describes as 'a long, hard, worthwhile grind.'

One local issue in that corner of North London was the Northern Irish question – we were only five years into that immiserating conflict and the prestige of the IRA was higher among London Irishmen than it is today. There were a number of local Irish clubs. The Conservative candidate visited them for discussions, these in his usual litotic style, he calls 'quite lively'. He very much disliked the IRA and said so. He would have another chance on 7 February 1991 to exercise his sang-froid against lively Irishmen.

On the main issue of the February election Major does not pretend to vividly original views different from the drift of his party. He had nothing against the miners then on strike but thought Arthur Scargill, calling shots from South Yorkshire, a bluffing bully whose arrogance had made him too big for his boots. He was not significantly responsive to the Enoch Powell view, a benchmark of the ideological right, that printed money had begotten the inflation with the passive miners merely its symptom.

Another issue particularly big in St Pancras North, was Edward Heath's Housing Finance Act of 1972, mild enough by Thatcher's standards. It was intended to put revenue accounts in order by increasing tenants' rents rather a lot but recycling the money for improvements, which that lady would have thought too good for them. But big rent increases in areas like Camden created uproar. The bill was the biggest issue of the campaign locally. Like Sue Winter, Major also recalls a certain vividness of personality in parts of the local Labour Party to the point where a police presence and protection were envisaged for the count even though it would give Labour a majority of 7,000.

Recollections of that campaign are on the whole warm. With his own supporters and the canvassed public he was according to Ms Winter very popular. 'It is very unusual to get a candidate whom everyone adores – there's always somebody who likes to dig a knife in.' But not here evidently. He was also to find time for something outside the constituency. Gerald Bowden, now MP for Dulwich, remembers, as a South Bank Poly teacher, having persuaded him to speak to students about Housing. 'I fully expected him to cry off from that particular date. I and everybody else would have done so in the circumstances. However, John honoured his standing commitment coming from north London to talk to a bunch of students in south London. There could be no possible electoral or publicity benefit.'

Major would also maintain the St Pancras contact, going back to speak there when he was Chancellor. 'This,' says Sue Winter, 'was not the sort of candidate who when talking to you seemed to be looking with one eye over your shoulder for somebody more important.' He was however 'always banging on about cricket, he could be very boring about it.'

He was also particularly thoughtful in handling her, ten years younger, a totally inexperienced agent, and for this reason annoyingly getting more national publicity from the papers than he was. 'He treated me as boss, realizing that a candidate has to be subordinate to the agent. All agents know that candidates are just tactical necessities and that you don't need a real human being. But,' she adds, 'there are many candidates who would walk all over a young agent instead, like him, of doing what he was told.' Again, when she fell ill with arthritis shortly after the election she found him a regular and caring visitor in hospital.

Another story of this campaign, related by Major to Sue, concerned an attempt, one wet day, to reach a recalcitrant constituent through the letterbox, something which was not uncommon. He rang the bell, a voice said, 'Who is it?' to which he answered, 'John Major, your Conservative candidate. I am canvassing you on behalf of the party, I hope I can count on your vote next week.' The voice repeated, 'Who is it?' Major said the same set of words again and received the same enquiring answer. After a third exchange he looked through the letterbox and saw first, a cage, then a parrot!

She speaks of him as one of the hardest workers she has ever known, but very reluctant to make use of publicity, saying, 'Well if people want to find out about me they can.' But she was aware of an element of nervousness as well as ambition beneath the mild exterior, a nervousness evident at the count.

Jock Stallard also has recollections of the election and his opponent. Now *Lord* Stallard, following Michael Foot's sensible plan for getting 'working peers', men with active life left to replenish Labour's thin ranks of scarlet, he recalls Major with regard but no special fuss. 'He seemed a perfectly pleasant young man. We didn't have a joint meeting, I've always followed the old principle "Why give the Tories a free platform when you hold the seat?"' Naturally he sees the constituency and his own local party in a different light to the Tory agent. 'Nasty? Certainly not. We were a touch lively perhaps.' He has no thought of having been particularly hostile or aggressive himself.

If I may with some experience of elections interpose a judgment, the Winter/Stallard contradictions are a classical form of mutual misunderstanding. Many older Labour politicians combine innate reasonableness in substance with a specialized line of blood-and-sand oratory. I would guess that Stallard, without the least tincture of personal ill will, will have denounced Major as a monster in human form. Sue as a young agent will have taken what only sounds like assault and battery, as assault and battery.

But this constituency for its former member is the classic Labour Camden where Barbara Castle and other notables actually lived, where even gentrification was of the kind that brought sociology lecturers into flats. He describes a piece of North London Left territory where the old working class, represented here by a combatative Scot, were aggressively sure of their rights and where the better-off suburban fringe had a full salting of beards and protest. The distinct impression of John Major for them is of a ship which passed in the night sounding its horn on a mute.

From the tone of his election address, Major knew the score exactly and returned the compliment: '*Since 1945 St Pancras North has persistently elected Labour candidates to Parliament. During this time St Pancras North has declined as a place in which to live.*' 'Persistently' is a nice word. It has distinct overtones of the courts – as in 'persistent offenders' or 'persistent refusal to pay maintenance.' It carries a reproof not to be offered to people likely ever to *desist* and elect you. St Pancras North was in effect his coaling station; he would put in a stop here to acquire credentials and embellish his CV. No longer would that document tell selection committees that they faced only a former youngest ever Housing chairman, they were to be offered a former parliamentary candidate.

The address for February 1974 carries a variant of the standard Heath catastrophe prose: '*We face two crippling threats to our future – industrial anarchy and inflation. These problems are worsened by the Labour and Communist parties encouraging each and every strike. This must stop! That is why we have an election.*'

All over Britain with varying degrees of conviction, Conservative candidates were reflecting the wrought and dramatic tone of Mr Heath's own mood after turning a dodgy predicament into a nervous crisis. But despite the reference to the Communist Party, there is no attempt in this otherwise understated and calm document to call up panic. A pinch of incense is dropped at the altar of crisis, but despite a weakness for initial capitals, there is no tabloid shriek here. Ever a believer in detail and rational discourse, Major sticks here to the 'Fight against Inflation' best summed up in its opening sentence: *'Inflation means rising prices and a fall in the value of your money. It is a social evil.'* Recent journalistic comment finds Major distressingly low key and he could indeed turn general conflagration into an unpleasant little flare-up. But given the general discredit in which the fraught mood and manner of 1974 now stands, a failure by a candidate to threaten apocalypse looks rather creditable.

In his address Major, photographed with darker hair than now and a pair of half-frame glasses upon which time and good taste have both made changes, raises five basic issues: inflation, pensions, housing, education and the Labour Party. The housing section though local is the most interesting, reflecting his own knowledge of the subject and quickly acquired local expertise. It also looks forward to something the Tories would do in a very big way. *'Tenants at Lissenden Mansions, Highgate, have prepared a scheme – the Lissenden Formula, that would enable them to buy their homes from the council and jointly manage others on the Estate.* THIS SCHEME CAN WORK, AND IS IMPORTANT. *It should be a blueprint for tenant participation elsewhere.'*

In local matters an individual candidate otherwise reciting the Lord's Prayer of the manifesto, can give some indication of his own interests. A Major keen on a house-buying electorate was slightly ahead of the Heath consensus and one might leap to call him a prospective hard Thatcherian. But it is just worth remembering that from the battery of Thatcher-labelled policies of 1979–91, council house purchase is one of the handful of hard successes. So its early advocate is equally entitled to claim a wise eclecticism.

On the topic of pensions however he argues: *'During six years of Labour rule they rose by only 20%. In half that time the Conservatives have increased Pensions by 55%. Despite inflation Pensioners are better off.* THIS IS STILL NOT GOOD ENOUGH.'

He goes on to speak of the Tories adopting a six-monthly uprating of pensions and other long-term benefits (this of course reflected the inflation Mr Heath had failed to stop). But along with a second point about the over eighties pension, he also reflects the Heath government's broad acceptance of welfare as a subject for pride. The emphasis is distinct.

On the personal side Major lists the standard information but tells us that he joined the Conservative Party in 1959 and mentions the infant candidacy of 1964. He also makes a suitably realistic assessment of his chances in this arena: '*John Major would like to take up that fight now. He may fail to. But he will certainly fight hard to succeed. Why not give him a chance?*'

It was – in February as subsequently in that year's second election in October – an expectation without hope of fulfilment. Once the February election was over with a further election likely at any time, given Harold Wilson's exiguous majority, Major occupied an anomalous position *vis-à-vis* his local party, though one which suggests excellent understanding between candidate and association. He was wanted for re-adoption but licensed to rove in pursuit of a more hopeful seat. At Paddington where Labour had a majority of just 1,000, he was shortlisted but lost to Mark Wolfson, now MP for Sevenoaks. He and Norma also went down to Portsmouth North whose selectors Norma found bossy and disagreeable and where Peter Griffiths, the Nigger Neighbour man, formerly of Smethwick, having stood once, was chosen again. There was also a whirl in Dorset, territory of the Salisburys for half of which Lord Cranborne sat, he was not chosen as companion piece to Bob the Heir.

After that Major decided to stay with St Pancras North for the October contest. In his October address, an altogether more sophisticated sheet, he does not repeat the formula. Nor does that October letter repeat the Curriculum Vitae. Instead, on the right-hand panel of the fold he prints five letters from constituents, often succinct and ungainsayable: '*Thank you for your successful effort in getting David into our local primary school.*' Or there is from 'Pensioner Islip Street NW5' '*Thank you for all you have done on our behalf. I have heard this morning that I have a rebate of £1.10 a week. Thank you very much.*'

Already Major was playing to strengths which he would put to full use in Huntingdon – and despite his genuine diffidence about flash publicity, he was shrewdly taking proper credit for the plain and practical things he was good at and which mattered to the public. The five letters – on pensions, school places, rubish collection and a housing move – suggest truthfully, a hardworking, effective problem-crunching technician – not bazooka politics and somewhat low on bazazz but useful to constituents.

In the middle panel he makes short comments on social services, education, law and order, housing rates and transport. On the first, *'Our social services still fail to provide adequately for many of the people most in need. I will campaign for better facilities for the mentally sick, the crippled, the blind and deaf . . . These people need our priority help and must have it.'*

On education he calls for *'real choice'*, *'more power for parents to send children where they want.'* (This last was a big point under certain stroppy Labour authorities.) Interestingly, he demands the abolition because of 'its bigotted policies', of the ILEA, then increasingly left wing, as it no longer was when actually abolished by Margaret Thatcher!

On law and order, he is Major the minimalist. *'This is a matter of great concern . . . We cannot allow this. I shall support the strengthening of the Police Force so that they can stamp out this trend.'*

On housing he not surprisingly, opposes *'The Labour Council's plans for total municipalization of housing'* (those were the days). It was *'forcing young people away from the Borough and denying homes of their own to many families who have always lived in Camden'*. This was good, sensible if re-active stuff from the days when Labour local authority initiatives had the power to scare people.

On transport he is sensibly local. Chalk Farm and Highgate, badly served, would press for improved local services *'to be run by London Transport or Private Enterprise'* (again those Teutonic capitals).

But it was on rates (or Rates) that like many Tories of this time, Major found himself contributing to the vocabulary of dramatic irony. The future member of the losing side majority faction against the Poll Tax in Cabinet, reasonably in 1974 criticized 'the totally outdated' domestic rating system which had 'led to enormous rate demands in Camden.' Less wisely but typically he then stated that Conservatives would *'abolish domestic rating within a normal parliament. We shall replace them by a more broadly-based tax related to peoples' ability to pay.'*

In their third parliament of 1987 the Conservatives would abolish domestic rating and replace it against the firm advice of the Chief Secretary, with a flat-rate impost which, starting riots and donating votes to charity, would destroy the Prime Minister of the day.

The main message of the address still concerned the crisis. Although it used some Heathian harrumph '*the gravest crisis since the war*' and '*the success or failure of the government will determine the quality of our whole way of life*', it is still temperate and characteristically stresses 'no glib promises'. Available as Major's leg is for pulling with that of 624 other Tory candidates on the great rates confusion, his communication with the voters during the ghostly ritual of fighting the unwinnable is sane, calm and full of proficient detail. There isn't a word in it that does him real discredit. How many candidates can claim as much seventeen years on?

Despite such exertions and improved professional skills his recollections of the second campaign are gloomy and sceptical, speaking only of its total boringness 'knowing you would lose, going over a campaign which, nationally, had been both lost and exhausted.'

Nationally of course circumstances were set against the Tories for five years. Jock Stallard's victory in February was part of the odd tentative swing to Labour, begotten out of exasperation with Heath's equestrian dithering. He had indicated through a Judge's arbitration the route to the inflationary increase which he had called the election to resist. Stallard's quiet second victory was part of the general disinclination of the voters to replicate for Harold Wilson the second ballot confirmation trick he had pulled off in 1966 – 'You know we are good chaps but we don't have the numbers to really govern properly. Let's have an extra margin on trust before we can do the sort of silly thing which would have you swinging back to the other lot.'

For a nation which gives an excellent impression of walking around in a political daze, the electorate had managed to vote with great shrewdness, rejecting two plausible if meritless ploys by two opposing politicians and coming down in favour of a national agnosticism very creditable in the circumstances. We voted for Labour on a ten-inch lead.

It was now with St Pancras North blessedly done full duty and hopes of winnables proffering their selection committees, that Central Office was to bring off another coup. For a considerable time Major put in applications in all directions and received at tepid best intimations that he should not trouble himself.

It was Jean Lucas, his guardian in Lambeth who, playing pop on his behalf, again came to the rescue of his career. A force in South London, she wanted to know of Putney Association why her boy had not been listed and was told he was not well enough qualified. Looking at the forms, she had the blinding experience of seeing that the credentials given were not *his* credentials. There was another John Major, a GLC member with only a tenuous interest in a Commons career who had not amassed the various Brownie badges of chairman of this, political officer of that, not to say two parliamentary candidacies, of our John Major. Central Office with a genius out of farce had, by confusing the two, helped to indicate a future Prime Minister as not worth the preliminary interview.

Central Office having been sorted out, Major was indeed invited to Putney and shortlisted there, meeting for the first time the eventual winner and MP, David Mellor, now Chief Secretary, who has been a close friend ever since. But he decided to forgo it, preferring his chances at the by-election-pending seat of Carshalton which would be taken in fact by Nigel Forman. But two months later he would face selection at Huntingdon where Norma Major was certain he would win. She had been brought up not far from there and it was, as she remembered and John did not, the anniversary of his selection five years before at St Pancras. She felt in her bones that he was going to win. Logically, you could find faults in her reasoning, but she was dead right.

5

Huntingdon

A group of Conservative activists in Huntingdon was far from happy at the prospective candidate their local association had finally chosen in 1976 to fight the next election. When he emerged from the room in which the members of the shortlist had effectively been detained, a prominent lady member of the committee actually avoided shaking hands with him, saving herself the humiliation of expressing public congratulations.

This was still *Huntingdonshire*. It would not become mere Huntingdon until a later re-drawing of boundaries – and this faction had distinct ideas about the sort of candidate it wanted. The collective heart of the faction was set on the Marquess of Douro, heir of the Duke of Wellington.

The tradition of Huntingdonshire as they saw it, was that of a county seat which should be represented by a county person. Charles Douro (later for a term a member of the European Parliament at Strasbourg) was happy to function as a working politician and was not to blame for other people's social aspirations. He was, however, perfectly equipped to meet them.

A descendant of the Iron Duke and heir to the Duchy of Wellington, he awaited the titles of Viscount Wellesley in Ireland and 12th Earl of Mornington (England), both dating from 1760, and 13th Baron Mornington, created in 1746, Prince of Waterloo, Duque de Victoria, Marques De Torres Vedras, Conde de Vimeiro – all in the peerage of Portugal; while the Spanish exertions of the first Duke had reserved to him the rank of Duque de Ciudad Rodrigo from 1812 and left him a Grandee of Spain (First Class).

The Marquess, also the patron of four livings in the Church of England, had been created for a committee lady's happiness and the Hunts Conservatives had chosen a man with a south London accent and a job in a bank. This is perhaps the point to publish the actual application made by John Major and submitted by him to Huntingdonshire constituency:

John Roy Major, Associate of the Institute of Bankers of 26 West Oak Avenue Beckenham Bromley; born 29 March 1943, married Norma Johnson, one daughter one son, Elizabeth and James, education Cheam Primary, scholarship to Rutlish Grammar, Associate of Institute of Bankers, Member National Union of Bank Employees. Previous employment: 1959–64 Industrial sculptor, '64 entered international banking, '67 seconded to Nigeria during Biafran war, '68–9 Foreign exchange dealer, '70–72 senior officer business development Africa responsible for advising on trade and economic conditions and capital investment overseas, '75 appointed senior business development executive Standard Charter Bank Britain's largest Overseas Bank.

Lectures frequently at Chambers of commerce CBI seminars, widely travelled throughout Far East and Africa. Voluntary work: member management board, warden housing association and warden second housing association. '75 President Fulham Taverners Cricket. '68–70, a school governorship. '69–70 member a Housing Centre Trust. Parliamentary; '71–4 candidate St Pancras North. Feb and October '74 contested unsuccessfully St Pancras North. As candidate '71–4 held weekly advice bureaux throughout constituency, held periodic public meetings, spoke at many organisations and schools. Established contacts with tenants and residents associations and other interest groups, contributed guest column to local newspaper. '64 contested borough council in Lambeth, '68 elected councillor Lambeth, member Housing committee, Chairman accounts committee, vice-chairman Housing committee.

'69 chairman Housing Committee, youngest in living memory in Lambeth. As Chairman presided over pioneer housing advice centre since copied throughout the UK. Initiated the policy of selling council houses and new homes to occupiers displaced in council redevelopments. Initiated public meetings at which councillors and officers answered electors' questions.

Constituency: Joined Tory party 1960. '60–64 Treasurer, Vice Chairman, Political officer, chairman Brixton Young Conservatives, '65 founder chairman Lambeth Borough YCs. '65–7 Chairman Association CPC committee. '68 constituency Treasurer, '69 constituency vice chairman, '70–71 Constituency Chairman to dissolution of association following Boundary Commissioners' report '75 branch-chairman Beckenham constituency association.

Miscellaneous: '68 member Central Office Speakers Panel, author: contributed to Conservative Party publications on Social Security and Housing. Has travelled extensively covering housing and other problems notably USSR, Finland and Holland.

Secondary points added. In 1976 attended IMF conference as personal assistant to Lord Barber. Interests: reading, cricket, music especially opera.

Despite the last throw with Lord Barber's patronage and a decent interest in Opera, this catalogue of solid, useful, socially applied, busy concern and activity is as remote from the less strenuous life pattern of most people as it is from that of Lord Renton or indeed the Marquess of Douro. It is, despite Major's esteem for Mrs Thatcher, not quite her style either. The selectors of Huntingdonshire were being offered someone who did believe that there was such a thing as society, and whose two shining passions, evident here, were housing and consultation with the general public.

The tone of the outline is post-Beveridge and in specifically Tory terms, post-Macleod. It shows no chips of resentment, makes no self-made-man boasts though he is precisely self-made. It suggests, along with social concern, a singularity of purpose in filling every inconsequential job in the local hierarchy of his party. As for roots, they are not even snubbable until that last flicker in Beckenham as 'suburban'. Many things can be said about Brixton and Lambeth but 'suburban' is not one of them!

To those who yearned for a county member with a sense of what was due to the ruling class and a regard for authority, it was not encouraging. Lord Willoughby De Broke in his memoirs *The Passing Years* describes the very different order which had held 'undisputed and comfortable sway' in his Victorian youth. In descending import-ance it constituted the Lord Lieutenant, the Master of Foxhounds, the agricultural landlords, the Bishop, the MPs, the Dean, the Archdeacon, the Justices of the Peace, the lesser clergy and the larger farmers. The Conservative Party had served one order, it now served another and would be represented in Parliament by a former London borough councillor with no social connections of any kind but a steady job in a bank and a proven dedication to social problems. We do in our way have revolutions.

Prejudice was not perhaps all on one side: 'I wasn't having the Marquess at any price whatever his ability,' remarks one fiercely democratic lady, active in the Association. The appeal of Mr Major on that occasion lay for his experience in the non-armigerous world of local government. 'We were,' says one official of the time, 'very impressed that he had been chairman of housing in Lambeth at twenty-six'. Another colleague adds that 'Ten or fifteen years ago someone like that wouldn't even have been considered.'

The constituency was changing out of all recognition. It would not be a shire much longer. The business overflow from the Cam-bridge high tech labs was already on flow, the twenty years from 1970 would see twenty-five business parks established. Huntingdon was attracting population overflow from London, and smaller local sources. The numbers were going up. The constituency had 39,000 members shortly after the war, by the time of the 1982 redrawing of boundaries it had 102,000 and had to be drastically cut down losing St Neots, proceeding thereafter to continue cheerfully increas-ing its numbers within the narrower boundaries.

The three key towns of St Ives, Godmanchester and Huntingdon itself contained everything from highly traditional silver-smithing and Chivers Jams to Brights, makers of the most sophisticated medical instruments, to the latest remarkable thing clever chaps can do with silicon. It also contained, ironically for its future MP and member of a watchdog organization against abuse of vivisection, Huntingdon Laboratories, the largest medical researchers by way of animal testing in Europe.

But these statistical facts understate the Montague-Capulet nature

of relations inside the constituency. Incomers and local residents
were divided roughly fifty fifty. One eyewitness speaks of bright,
sharp youngsters from London confronted by country people with
a county leadership in which Commander Archie Gray, Chairman
in the year of Major's selection, and his wife were joined by Sir
Peter Crossman and other landowners. Sherry parties given by the
Grays constituted a thin bridgehead between the groups, and in a
very British way, the sort of bridgehead from which many people
felt excluded.

Andrew Thompson who had lately come to the town, a man who
would also see service as Margaret Thatcher's agent in Finchley,
speaks of the great need in the town for reconciliation, healing even.
Huntingdon was in the process of becoming a New Town almost
under the meaning of the act, worried about jobs in the early 1970s
but destined, as the jobs came, to worry more about housing and
expansion.

It was not the seat David Renton had inherited at the end of the
War. Lord Renton, as he became, had been a good member, concerned with such matters as mental health and trade union law. His
career which had not taken him above Minister of State level, was
thought by friendly judges to have understated his abilities, the
cards simply turning unluckily. Renton had lately in the mid-seventies become depressed by the House of Commons. He particularly
disliked the raucous hard left, notably Dennis Skinner and had
grown weary.

His conduct throughout proceedings to find a successor was
strictly correct. He indicated no preferences, attempted to pull no
strings, but was keen to act to his successor as studio master to
apprentice. The relationship was to be a useful one with the young
man from the Standard Charter Bank attending a wide range of
functions and helping with many duties.

However, that said, whatever his merits, Renton, first elected in
1945, belonged comprehensively to an elder generation. His final
speech in the constituency as retiring member, as reported by the
Hunts Post, reads like a parody of the knighted backbencher as seen
through the eyes of John Wells:

*Lower moral standards, the growth of crime and divorce and the permissive
society caused more unhappiness than fulfilment. There was less censorship*

and a decline in religion, loyalty did not seem to be as important as it was, which he regretted very much. Worst of all, egalitarianism had produced a contempt for authority. There must be a respect for leadership and indeed more leadership in a stable society.

He would be happy if we saw a sign of the revival of national greatness. We had lost an empire and our economic fortunes had declined. They would not revive until we stopped bickering and restored respect for authority and stopped trying to get higher incomes than we were prepared to work for. All MPs found that constituency demands were always increasing. They feel that people ought to refer their problems to local councillors. Work had always been heavy but now the scope had been greatly increased; this had led to more committee work. The Labour Party was better educated but more left wing. The Conservatives had a broader social base without losing contact with the ruling class.

He was in favour of immigration controls and was a progressive on education and felt strongly about defence. Heath could not have remained as leader because he had lost three out of four elections. He did not believe that Mrs Thatcher was a reactionary. But the national press had been venomous. In education Mrs Thatcher was progressive. The idea of encouraging people to stir up interest and controversy was unrealistic. As to his successor, John Major, he had no doubt he would win with a good majority.

When all the civilities are uttered, this is the peevish, selfish speech of an old man resenting the present indicative tense. Its references to 'the ruling class', and respect for authority and its resentment of the work asked of MPs by constituents coming with their troubles is as remote as Alpha Centauri from everything John Major, from his 'wider social base', represents. It is a miserable complaint about the failure of other people to behave conveniently. John Major's chief felicity in politics, the arts of not quarrelling and staying on good terms with all kinds of difficult persons must have finally graduated from the two-year course of dutiful co-existence with Sir David, though he says nothing but kind and grateful things about Renton and his late wife, Paddy.

But in selection itself Renton by every account, consciously and rightly, played no part. The only guidance (very good guidance) offered by anyone to the selectors came from the Chairman, Archie Gray. (He was a retired naval commander and very well liked.) 'With this seat, safe as it is and near enough to London as it is, you don't want to settle for anything less than a prospective Cabinet Minister,' he advised. Survivors of the '76 selection believe that they had occupied themselves with such notions of coolly seeking merit when they sifted the applications – 320 of them as Roger Juggins, later Chairman himself, recollects.

The Marquess, who at least made it to the short list, did better than Peter Lilley, now Trade Secretary and member for St Albans, or the late Keith Wickenden. Lilley recollects meeting on an uptrain as he was waiting for a down one, somebody instantly recognizable by double-breasted dark suit and furtive expression, as an interviewee for the preliminary selection process. 'I tried to give him various bits of bad advice,' he recalls of the Prime Minister, 'but he was obviously much too shrewd to follow it.' Wickenden, Chairman of Euro-Ferries, was eliminated by way of the A, B and C lists, upon which sifting committees sat and largely squashed.

Christopher Patten, now Chairman of the Conservative Party, found wanting and superfluous, was deleted before the short list was made. He has had to make do with Liberal Democrat-assailed Bath, now made dodgy and marginal by the depredations of a Uniform Business Rate vividly inimical to its many shops.

The short list for the final day was made up of John Major, Alan Haselhurst, the Marquess Douro and Jock Bruce-Gardyne. All would have careers of some sort, Douro briefly in Strasbourg and Haselhurst from 1977 as MP for Saffron Walden, by-elected after the wretchedly early death of Peter Kirk. Bruce-Gardyne (formerly Member for South Angus) would return for a term and minor Treasury office as MP for Knutsford in Cheshire. He died in 1990 in his late fifties – of a brain tumour heroically encountered and resisted.

If the Conservatives of Huntingdonshire were following a measure of class-factionalism, and disposed in the majority for distinctly gritty and meritocratic candidates, then Major apart, only Haselhurst would really have suited them. Very hardworking and scrupulous, solid middle middle class by background, King Edward VI Birmingham and Oxford, he is perhaps a whit too serious. But as a steadily consistent liberal Tory, has been denied the office he thoroughly deserves. And if the Marquess whose main fault was want of true lust for politics, would have encountered social discrimination, Jock Bruce-Gardyne would have exercised it! A deer stalker and salmon fisher on the great estates, a man of formidable intellect, gracefully disdainful of voice and inclined to an umbrella-in-ribs manner, he was given to speaking of 'oiks', 'dear little men' and, in the case of Falkland islanders, 'sheep-shaggers'.

He was also given to voicing the 'K' in the name of his subsequent constituency. The electors of K-nutsford, given the chance in the boundary Commission redrawings of 1982, saw to it that none of the three successor seats taking up its parts, chose Bruce-Gardyne. A Wykhamist, he had lived up to the evaluation of Herbert Wilson, father of Harold, who having met Douglas Jay, Hugh Gaitskell and Richard Crossman in one soul-erasing afternoon, remarked that he now knew where God had been to school.

Courage, excellent brains, good humour among his intellectual peers, and an independence of mind which would lead him to a healthy contempt for the penny whistle jingoism of the Falklands War, never offset a scorn, largely reflexive, for the not-brilliant, the commonplace or for dear little people generally. He went through a too short life belittling others and talking himself out of the place and active role his gifts required.

A hopeful sign for Major shortly before the final selection took place was the prophecy of Crossbencher in the *Sunday Express* who announced that the obvious winner was Bruce-Gardyne with the Marquess as the next most hopeful runner. Major, added Cross-bencher, didn't have a chance. 'That,' he says, 'made me feel a lot better since I know their form.'

The contest between the candidates followed alphabetical order. Neither Douro nor Bruce-Gardyne were particularly strong. But Andrew Thompson speaks rapturously of the Haselhurst con-tribution: 'A marvellous speech, I was making a note for my con-gratulations to "the new member".' 'Then,' he says, 'John got up and he just swept the board, an incredible speech.' 'What was it about?' 'Healing, reconciliation; he knew there were problems between communities and he spoke to that.'

After the speeches and while the selectors went to work, John and Norma slipped out for a drink, the particulars of which Major oddly enough remembers; tomato juice for him; orange juice for her. 'Alcohol just didn't seem the order of the day.' He confirms what I had heard elsewhere that on the way back they heard 'a terrific cheer' and saw the upraised arms of a lady who had earlier, against Queen's regulations, let him know not only that she supported him but that support was running high with people who liked his local government/London background. She had advised him to stick to the line he had taken in his two earlier interviews and was not to think of Huntingdon as a county town only. Effectively he knew he had won and Commander Gray confirmed the fact. 'You've all done extremely well but I must congratulate *you*,' at which he took John Major's hand.

The result had been to the point, no second ballots or votes to transfer. Out of 186 votes cast John Roy Major had received 109.

Both Majors had reason for being emotionally overwhelmed, something worked for widely but not quite expected here had happened. The parliamentary life was opening up. Major, though, with his usual dislike of the dramatic, simply said, 'It's a long way from Brixton to Huntingdon, but it all seems worthwhile.' To Jo Johnson, a future close constituency friend, he confided even less triumphantly, 'I think that I can see light at the end of the tunnel.' Norma, whose red dress had been mildly remarked at, was quietly rocked by the enormity of it all and said that she couldn't take in what had happened. There was a mill of people, much meeting and then the Majors drove home. They did not celebrate in the customary champagne fashion of many politicians of all parties. There was no dinner at a smart place to be seen at, but when next day a salesman tried to sell them one, they bought their first microwave cooker which they still have. The snubbing classes will shriek at that, but it actually seems the action of a citizen.

The result at the Commemoration Hall had had its foundations laid in earlier questionings during the siftings. Major had done himself no harm by one candid declaration of ignorance. He was asked about his view on 'Country sports', as men with twelve bores call shooting and its like. 'Oh,' he said, 'I didn't expect that one. I don't know anything at all about them. I can't give a proper answer until I do.' This astute ignorance, which extended to most things agricultural, was a better option than defiant urban dislike, ready and ingratiating compliance or the furtiveness into which many of us would take flight.

As for not knowing about agriculture, Roger Juggins remarks, 'I took care of that.' Across six months, he adds, Major grasped all the essentials. 'He didn't have to be able to calve a cow, but the things he needed to know he grasped very fast.'

The electors had taken Major to them, partly by his CV – two brave efforts in St Pancras against Jock Stallard and his majority and hard work on a real subject, housing – principally though because of the quickness and clarity of his mind. 'No beating about the bush or flapping about,' said Olive Baddeley, the present Association Chairman, 'and he's stayed like that.' His answers to questions about the economy and union power at that selection were quick and concise. But involvement with local government also mattered.

Speaking to his partisans one gets a distinct impression that the country tradition of Independents rather than candid Tories standing for the council is disliked for the same reasons as the search for a county candidate. 'They used to like "men of goodwill",' said one constituency officer with some scorn. This seemed to its critics the mechanism of a clique. Major's uncomplicated record of enthusiastic borough councilling as a straight Tory in Lambeth where goodwill is likely to be served as left-cross to the jaw, was seen as modern, urban and relevant.

There is no escaping the impression that the Conservatives who chose the Prime Minister for his seat fourteen years ago, wanted a specific and spelt-out break from the rural paternalist (and toad-eating) tradition. David Renton is spoken of with respect for decency and competence, but the fact that this young man was not public school or indeed university, that he had a share of the squashed whistle of South London in his speech, that he did a solid but unprivileged and not particularly high-flying job in a bank, that unlike Douro he was not attached to a German Princess, a descendant of Kaiser Wilhelm, but to a nice woman in the wrong colour dress, must all have been positive advantages to him.

It says something that his unhesitating opposition to the death penalty, raised several times – during the sifting and on the short list – did him no great harm. (Haselhurst is a flat opponent, while Bruce-Gardyne, while not supporting that penalty, would cynically voice support and vote for it in the Commons to appease K-nutsford. It would be fascinating to know how he answered that night).

Major had also helped himself by a categoric readiness to move to the constituency if chosen. This eagerness was proof of him wanting them badly and unconditionally enough for them to want him. He and Norma found a house in Hemmingford Grey, a village five miles from Huntingdon on the Cambridge Road. And established, after sale and purchase delays, at De Vere Close, he became, in contrast to his rail-hating leader, a commuter travelling weekly to and from London and the bank job on the King's Cross trains – today 'forty-three minutes for the good ones, about an hour for the not so good,' but at that time much less frequent. He would later move to his present house in Great Stukeley.

Chequers has been reserved for special occasions but 'Finings' will not easily accommodate a visiting head of state. 'It has a couple of acres but, that apart,' says Jo Johnson, 'nothing grand, an ordinary detached suburban house. Mind you the kitchen is nice – better than Downing Street.' Was it then particularly magnificent? 'No,' she says, adding very Scottishly, 'but I've seen them both, and as for the one at Downing Street, Och, *I* wouldn't have it!'

His early days as a candidate were demonstrative of a nice democratic style. Taken to the racecourse in which Huntingdon takes some pride and generally introduced, he shook hands with everyone including, at his insistence, the man hired to shovel up muck behind the horses. The faintly Jacobin desire for a candidate beneath or above grandeur and willing to perform, was satisfied in spades. He was in the constituency every weekend, doing a surgery, always available at the wide range of small socials in which the Conservative Party wisely specializes and with which diffuse constituencies with lots of villages, quite overflow.

As a candidate, he was helped by Andrew Thompson and David Renton to get himself proper links with business. Renton had run a small dining club called the Huntingdon Industrial Forum. Big farmers were much involved. Not yet fully briefed by Roger Juggins, Major was uneasy about how to handle them. His agent was breezily practical. 'It's business, John, farming is business. You know all about that from banking. Talk business to them.' He also plunged into making social acquaintance across the constituency. 'There might be six or eight gatherings across the county over a weekend,' says his agent. 'We'd split them: David Renton, his wife Paddy, Norma, me and John, crisscrossing the area to be in touch with everyone.'

This would remain his pattern even when in office and later the Cabinet. Neither pride of soul nor the especial grind of the Chief Secretary, required to grasp everyone else's department in order to count their money out, kept him from wine and cheese parties for twenty people in Alconbury or Little Gidding.

Roger Juggins recalls a very trying time as a minister when Major had been missing most of his sleep. 'It's only a little do for a dozen people at the other end of the constituency,' he had said. 'Let me explain to them that it just can't be done. . . . But no, he wasn't having that. Members had paid their one pound fifty or whatever it was then, and they expected the member to be available and he would be.

'So we get him into the car and he promptly falls asleep. Then on the way back after being attentive and friendly there, he went to sleep again. And when he got back and woke up he asked me in for a drink but I told him, "You just get straight up to bed." '

This attitude carries the ordinary attentiveness of sensible politicians to extreme lengths – and might best be seen as professionalism reinforced by natural good manners. It was demonstrated again on the Saturday after last November's hand-kissing call at the Palace. By ill luck two functions had been fixed in the constituency that evening, one in Gletton, the other in Bluntisham, ten miles either way from his home in Great Stukeley. 'I'd just do Bluntisham,' Roger said, 'that's plenty after such a week. "No, no," he says, "I'll do both. Just ask one of them to rejig the time by half an hour so that I can be there long enough." '

He was a trouble taker with his surgeries, looking for solutions and answers, spending quantities of time with callers. The tale is told (again by Roger) of Bill Carter: 'Rank Labour in those days, now he's John's biggest supporter. He had been made redundant and he had a big housing problem. John went through it with him, made some enquiries, and got something going, came back to it with Bill and kept at it till everything was settled right.' 'He doesn't like bureaucracy,' says Mrs Johnson. 'One of his phrases is, "This is a nonsense" and he'll say that when they come and tell him about some delay that he can sort out.'

The devotion could at election time become mild fussiness. He was so anxious, says Olive Baddeley. He worried about the Renton effect. It was reckoned Sir David had had a big personal vote and Major was terrified of losing it and slumping. He even worried about a surge in the Scottish Nationalists. Olive laughs. 'John,' I said, 'whatever else happens, the Scot Nats are not going to be big in Huntingdon.' He was and is a worrier and, in Mrs Baddely's words, 'hung around those tressell tables at the count like an expectant father'. 'He fought it,' said Andrew Thompson, 'like a marginal.'

Emily Blatch has an illustrative story of Major as a campaigner and his attention to detail. Then a local activist and later a councillor in Cambridgeshire, Emily Blatch was brought into government as a Minister in the Lords at Environment. 'His dream', she says, 'was to win that election by more votes than David Renton, his absolute dream was to get into five figures, ten thousand or above. I at the time was working at the association on jobs like postal votes, but after five thirty we would all go off booted and spurred and go canvassing. One day he said to me, "Emily, don't feel me impertinent but how do you manage for your children?" I replied, "it's only for three weeks and I have a lady who helps, Mrs Irvine, who understands and takes care of the children in the evenings." The next day I slipped home to replenish something in the larder. Mrs Irvine was excited. "I've got a letter, I've got a letter." It said, "Dear Mrs Irvine, You won't know me. My name is John Major. I am the parliamentary candidate for Huntingdon. I know that Emily who is being so helpful in the campaign would not be able to do so much for me if it wasn't for you. I want you to know how grateful I am to you".'

The perfect political manners which echo across his parliamentary and ministerial career operated at the height of an election campaign.

Lady Blatch has another intimation of the Major approach. He would have the canvassers make a note of any voter with a query or problem. It would be sorted from the returned cards and at least an hour a day would be given to responding to these questions at once. He had refined that system at successive elections and generally as an MP was exceptionally good at reacting to problems raised.

There would be an immediate holding letter, the acknowledgement, a search for information. People were so impressed, she said. He didn't make big private promises at elections but if he could chivvy up the council he would. This she thought made him very effective as a candidate, one couldn't canvass ninety thousand people, but party workers were not selling a candidate in a vacuum, what he could and would do quickly became known.

As a speaker locally she remembers him as a quick thinker on his feet, someone who enjoyed heckling and who could be punchy without nastiness. She tells the story of a local heavy loyal to Labour who attempted to walk ostentatiously out of a meeting only to step into a cupboard. 'It's alright,' Major said, 'you can come out now. I've changed the subject.'

She also has recollections of the count on election night 1979. This took place at the St Ivo's Centre in St Ives. 'The tables were laid out,' she said, 'and one by one the other parties came to an end of their votes, first the Greens, then Labour, while they had to fetch extra tables to accommodate his. But he was so hung up on this business of getting first a vote more than Renton, then if possible getting five figures that he asked when his line stopped, "Do you think they might have mislaid a box?" In fact he had fulfilled both ambitions.'

The majority had of course gone up. It had done rather more than that. Thompson, with an agent's knowledge of votes cast so far, recalls being misunderstood when commuting to an outer group he spoke of 20,000. 'That's not bad at all,' said somebody. David Renton didn't ever poll better than 23,000. When the result showed a *majority* of more than 21,563 the response was ecstatic.

As a Member of Parliament, Major made a number of policy speeches as well as committing himself on local issues. (Excitingly he refused in Parliament to join the Esperanto Group.) Much of his local utterance, as is inevitable in heavily disciplined British politics, tended to unexciting salutation of the government's high wisdom (this is not the life of a rebel). But on the broad drift of the economy what was said did constitute conviction as well as conformity. And certain Major qualities emerge – ready statistics certainly, but an inclination to argue about the quality of a public service.

Here he is on education. 'A beggarly one per cent of the education budget was spent on school books,' he told the Hinchingbrooke Society in the constituency in February 1981 defending cuts. The previous year's expenditure had been £7.5 billion, it would come down by £350 million. It couldn't be right that transport and meals should be the largest item of the budget taking ten per cent of the total expenditure. The first elements of education were quality and quantity of teachers, buildings and grounds and sufficient school books. Most people supposed these accounted for the bulk of spending, they didn't, salaries took up fifty-three per cent, buildings ten per cent, books less than one per cent. We spent three pence per child per week on books. The remaining thirty-five per cent went on administration, meals, agency costs, transport and cleaning. Cuts should fall in these areas. While he supported the right to private education overwhelmingly, money must go to improving the state system. He didn't think it impossible to make acceptable cuts in the cost of administration.

He was not convinced that local authorities were right to maintain their firm and detailed grasp of schools. It seemed to him that schools like Hinchingbrooke (a local comprehensive) were capable of almost entire self-government. There should be much more freedom for schools within the comprehensive system.

This was not prophetic of what would become the party's correct view of education which was to become increasingly centralized, untrusting of school heads and staff and decidedly peremptory. But it is perhaps more consistent with an outlook broadly liberal and unauthoritarian beyond stock market freedoms.

Early in his time in Huntingdon he was anxious to maintain contact with voters beyond the minima of surgery and election times. He instituted public consultation meetings. At one of these in 1980 he made a defence of the Government to sixty people in the town hall, a turnout the chairman was happy with since the competition that night was 'All Creatures Great and Small'. His case was couched in the orthodox monetarist language which would be dropped from the vocabulary by Nigel Lawson and then be recalled again. Money supply was all important. The national debt had risen from '74 to '79 from forty-two billion to eighty-seven billion. The interest alone on paying it off was £9 billion more than we spent on education, the health service or defence. Rather in the way of Mrs

Thatcher in her Symphonia Domestica style, he remarked that no one would buy a colour TV and leave it to his children to pay off. And in a fashion characteristic of Conservatives in those rough disemploying years, he warned that there was 'no need for a pall of gloom'.

The school of thought which today speaks of Major as 'a grey man' had its pre-echoes with the comment of the Huntingdon Liberal association's chairman who described Major as 'the identikit candidate,' his press contributions as 'press circulars from Central Office' and wished that 'we had an MP capable of original thought.'

In fact much of his pronouncement was directed locally to matters of vast significance to Fenland farmers. The hairs on the back of the broad public's neck do not stand rigid at the sugarbeet quota and the unspeakable things done to it by the Commission of the EC. But a politician surrounded horizon to horizon by a beet crop menaced by supply managers, makes speeches, asks questions for written answers and makes a decent show of concern. Major raised with the Agriculture minister threats to the beet quota threatened with a reduction of twenty-nine per cent. Mr Walker made soothing noises about matters under review and due for consultation.

More generally Major was drawn into argument about the Government's training schemes, about the utility of which more than one opinion exists. His comment was in the way of loyal assent from a backbencher, not startling or original, but it didn't cringe and its ring is sympathetic, an instructive mixture of two lifelong qualities, caution about spending money and attentive understanding towards the losers.

Asking local employers to become involved with the Youth Opportunities Scheme, the job position for youngsters, he said in October, was undoubtedly very serious. They were facing difficulties not of their own making. He couldn't emphasize too strongly that unemployed youngsters were not workshy or ill-educated, they were well educated and wanted to work but there are no jobs for them. It was not prudent, he said, Treasury style but sensibly, to create jobs which were not permanent or artificial. The solution must be an expansion of their experience through the Youth Opportunity programme. Local employers had nothing to lose and everything to gain because when the economy picked up, they might wish to employ permanently people encountered under the scheme.

Every Conservative backbencher will have said something in commendation of this particular nostrum, but for many of them it was privately seen either as a way to fudge the unemployment figures or as a form of doing-therapy: why isn't the Government doing something? It is, it has launched the Youth Opportunities Scheme. Major showed no such insouciance and what is noticeable about a routine piece of advocacy of party policy is that it is delivered from the point of view of the young people.

The great undertaking of Major as an MP was, however, concerned with Hinchingbroke hospital. A bigger problem was the parallel struggle to establish Huntingdon and its surrounds as a full health authority. The concern here was to fight off the magnetic pull of Addenbrooks, the great Cambridge hospital which too remote for Huntingdon was near enough to syphon off resources.

The new MP set to lobbying ministers, Gerard Vaughan then Health Minister, a former GLC member from South London though not known to Major, as well as Mrs Thatcher herself. The struggle continued, as it used to say on left-wing posters, from just before Major's first election until 1981 when both objectives – hospital and area status – were achieved.

The other important campaign involving Major heavily concerned the rail service between Huntingdon and King's Cross. Today, as one can vouch for from field experience, the service is good and frequent throughout the day. In Major's early days in the town, it was poor – two or three trains at peak hours in the morning, nothing from London after eight at night, not enough in the morning, little during the day, very little at weekends. Major spent time on the platforms doing surveys and then presented a case. In fact as he says it was a strong one. Huntingdon was a fast-growing town with large travel demands and the service was nothing like adequate. He is not certain that it was his campaigning which did the trick, but British Rail did respond and, as he lightly observes, he got the credit which in politics is all that counts.

Perhaps as instructive about Major as MP and his political colour as anything he did, was an attack on conditions in employment offices. On 22 January 1981 he sought in a ten-minute bill 'to improve archaic and humiliating conditions in the unemployment benefits office.' 'When people are made unemployed they have to register at such an office on the first day possible after becoming unemployed. If they do not they lose the benefit for the intervening period.

'Many people become unemployed on a Friday, so on Monday a lot of people turn up at the offices, all at 9 a.m. and may have to queue all day through 'till as late as four or five o'clock because there are only two or three clerks. This seems appalling to me because most of these offices are old and dull without chairs and lacking in privacy.'

He spoke of a queue on one occasion stretching right outside the office. When people were seen, they often found themselves being dealt with by clerks young enough to be their grandchildren, no chairs, only three clerks, no provision for running a ticket system to allow people to come back the next day. That is the sort of thing the department could bring in without difficulty. He was speaking about the Peterborough office, but he was not blaming anyone specifically, only the conditions. He was sure the clerks had done their best within the guidelines. Young clerks did a super job, but if you were a fifty-five-year-old married man having to queue four or five hours to give personal details to a young lady of eighteen years in semi-public, you wouldn't find it very pleasant. There was no privacy in these places.

Many people who had been made redundant because of the recession had worked for many years often in a senior position. It was bad enough without having to face all this. He was simply asking for more dignity. In all his visits he had been accompanied by a former employment minister (David Renton) who shared his view. He would keep a check on the matter to see if there was any response to these remarks in public, if not he would bring it up again.

This intervention, a brilliant demonstration by the way of how Parliament can be turned to account to shift a local wrong while firing shots at a wider injustice, is not the conventional speech of a Conservative backbencher. Where his remarks on the Youth Opportunities Scheme merely put a human gloss onto support for official policy, the attack on benefits office practices is concrete, it concerns the feelings and dignity of people not always credited with having the one or being entitled to the other. It is directed against bureaucracy and indifference and it makes an imaginative jump into the sensibilities of the man in the queue.

Everything Major's friends have said about him as councillor and minister is borne out here. It has exactly nothing to do with the Tory Right who would ensure his election as leader, people who at their best lack social empathy. It is close to the outlook of an outspoken Wet like Sir George Young, one of Major's great personal friends. But none of it could have quite been said by the most generous and kindly politician who had enjoyed higher education for ten years before entering steady employment. If Major had been sensible when he was sixteen, if he had gone to Cambridge or indeed Keele, had never been in a rough job or out of any job at all, if he had not stood in a dole queue himself, he could not have spoken in that heartfelt expert way. It is a simple call for elementary inexpensive decency achieved with a little trouble and organization. But how many MPs would have thought to make it?

In March 1981 the Conservative Government took its single most radical, driest and economically hardbitten step, the taking out of the economy of five billion pounds, something resisted in Cabinet by the Chancellor, Sir Geoffrey Howe, and promulgated by the Prime Minister in response to lobbying by Alan Walters and Keith Joseph. It marked a victory, at least for the time being, of the dry school, intensified deflation and disemployment but would make possible a fall in inflation to a low point of just over three per cent. Major's response as a constituency MP should be seen in the light of his much later remarks as Chancellor and Prime Minister about his hatred of inflation.

On 19 March of that year he spoke regretting the increase in petrol prices by twenty per cent; he would have preferred ten per cent. He applauded the introduction of a loan guarantee scheme. This was something which he had independently advocated wishing only that it had been bigger and funded above the given fifty millions. He praised tax changes as making investment in small business more likely. He did, however, regret the failure to maintain the index-linking of personal tax allowances. 'Failure to do so will reduce the income of every working family.'

Like many Conservatives he made obeissance to the bogey of

world oil prices. He struck a dry and realistic note by saying that old ailing industries could not be sustained, they no longer contributed to the national economy and must be weeded out. If this wasn't done we would continue to be a third rate declining power. A whole series of decisions had to be taken now which would be widely unpopular but would benefit our children in twenty years time. Wrongly but typically for the date, he forecast a retiring age of sixty by the end of the decade and a shorter working week. There would be a higher pool of unemployment and society must make arrangements to cope with it.

This response, though not unusual for an intelligent supporter of the Government while trying to keep bruised constituents happy, had nuances which help define Major. He greeted with delight the doubling of the blind allowance. This was something he had raised with the Chancellor publicly and urgently a few months before. The concession was something for a social purpose done with money and typical of Major's general social concern.

But his words about old industries could have come from the Adam Smith Institute or indeed the Thatcher Cabinet. The words used – 'no longer contributed to the economy, must be weeded out' – were crisp, there was no attempt to straddle, prevaricate or delude listeners. This was surgical talk. But no one has ever accused Major of brutality or enjoying necessary pain. He was speaking here surely as someone able unhesitatingly to grasp the unpleasantness of macro-economic decisions directed against subsidy and over-manning and against the idea of the Government as guarantor by inertia of major business in decline.

It was very much the speech of a future Treasury Minister, indeed of the Chancellor who would say, 'If it isn't hurting, it isn't working.' With respect to Major's future role as a minister acceptable to Mrs Thatcher personally, it made him on the key plank of unrelenting deflation, tight money and industrial pain, 'one of us'. The distinction between such attitudes and the care for social spending is a complication but not an inherent contradiction. The deflation of 1981 may have been overdone as the flight from tight money certainly was to be in 1987–8. Major's exact judgment may not have been wholly accurate but the reaction to the 1981 budget is not a toadying speech. Allowing for some constituency back-watching

over petrol prices which logically he should be saluting, it is intellectually freestanding and, distinguishing social care and industrial
subsidy, refines the profile of the man.

By contrast, his involvement in argument with unilateralists represented the standard view of every Conservative MP. The Amer-
icans had a base at Molesworth in Cambridgeshire into which in
1981 they moved cruise missiles. Speaking on a local Anglia TV
programme 'Members Only', Major debated with a local CND
officer, Adrian Howells, on 12 November 1981. Nuclear weapons
were necessary, he said, since Russians would not disarm if others
did, the peace process was damaged by anti-nuclear marches and
demonstrations. He followed this up with an intervention in Parliament on the adjournment making no apology for priority given
to defence, his constituents were totally resolute on the matter.
Disarmers and CND especially were presenting an utterly false
perspective to the country.

This as a contribution was entirely predictable. 'Conservative
supports introduction of cruise missiles' is as news, hardly even
'Dog bites man', more like 'Dog barks in sleep'. As a policy view
it was probably correct but as an illustration of a mind working it
doesn't begin to be interesting. Any Conservative MP can do this
with a stick and ball balanced on his nose. While the support
over the budget was private and nuanced, the line on defence was
handout-speak.

Generally he showed no special interest in foreign issues, but on
one occasion he was brought briskly into contact with a world crisis
at its rawest. Trips are arranged by an organization sympathetic to
Palestinian claims for MPs and journalists to travel very unluxur-
iously to the West Bank of the Jordan, Gaza and Arab Jerusalem.
They would stay, as an organizer put it, in $1\frac{1}{2}$-star Arab hotels. On
8 April 1982 Major joined one of these tours and came within
appreciable range of deletion from the living.

He went on this trip, said Major, because he knew very little
about the conflict; all he knew was the Israeli case. The party of
eleven MPs of all parties met the mayors of Ramallah and Nablus
the day after they had been deposed by the Israelis. The mayors
prophesied (wrongly) annexation of the West Bank by the Israelis
within weeks. They encountered charges that cash was being offered

to settlers to live on land recognized as Arab by international law. He saw refugee camps containing Arabs allegedly forced off their land by the Israelis.

The trip continued into Lebanon, at that time occupied in part by Israel. On the south coast, which had been 'flattened like a bombsite', near Sidon they could see a full-scale battle taking place a hundred yards away. In Beirut they were stopped by armed teenagers and outside their hotel a man was shot.

But the real action took place for the party at a place called Beit Ammar. 'Arab youths were throwing rocks at Israelis who were shooting at them.' One Arab youth threatened to throw a rock at the party. A guy told him who they were and he put it down. The youth went berserk when an Israeli car came towards them. He threw the rock at the car, missed and almost hit Major and Ken Weetch (then Labour MP for Ipswich). If it had been much closer, Major said there would have been a by-election in Huntingdon or Ipswich. Israelis began shooting at the youth, bullets went over and through the group of MPs (through the group, not the MPs). The incident, he added, only lasted a minute and a half, and they had no time to think of the danger. One story about this episode not reported in the local press involves an armed Israeli grabbing the Conservative MP, now Minister, Richard Needham and using his knee as a rest to steady the butt of his weapon.

The party went on more civilly to meet and talk with Mr Yasser Arafat. Major expressed to the PLO leader the standard Western views that the Organization should recognize that Israel had a right to exist (now agreed to) and said 'that Israel had no right to be on the West bank of the Jordan. There was a similar meeting with Crown Prince Hassan of Jordan.'

For a politician preoccupied with domestic detail, Major had concentrated a great deal of international education into a short span. Not many politicians are stoned or shot at, perhaps not enough. The requirement of having to throw themselves on the ground behind their vehicle to avoid being killed should be educative. Major's subsequent comment was decently chastened and he was ready to say that events generally in the West Bank were far more serious than he had realized, that people didn't understand what was happening, and he subsequently contacted the Foreign

Secretary and the Israeli Ambassador. Mrs Major speaking to the *Huntingdon Post* said that there was no point in panicking. John Major remarked however, that it had been the most exciting day of his life.

Being an MP would often be interesting, but rarely as interesting as this.

6

Parliamentarian

The Parliament which Major entered provided the new Conservative Government with a majority of forty. It was a rather hesitant administration with far to go before quiet confidence would seriatim replace nervousness before being followed by noisy confidence, triumphalism and paranoia.

At the last Thatcher Cabinet of 22 November 1990 no original colleague of the Prime Minister's in May 1979 was present. Sir Geoffrey Howe was a member, a cautiously deflationary Chancellor due to have his first bout with Sir Alan Walters before the Budget of 1981 when he would agree to taking five billion out of the economy. Otherwise it was a cabinet of Keith Joseph and John Biffen, Francis Pym and James Prior, Ian Gilmour and Norman St John Stevas, Lord Carrington and John Nott, Patrick Jenkin and Michael Heseltine.

Very few of its members left voluntarily and happily after a pleasant sufficiency of Government. Otherwise the list of the Cabinet is the list of traitors, deadbeats and other distortions of Mrs Thatcher's perception, who left in varying terms between masochistic acquiescence (Stevas) and scarlet sensation (Heseltine).

The Chief Whip in those days when the present Chief Whip and long-term Major friend, Richard Ryder, was a new member, was Michael Jopling, a spasmodically bonhomous farmer representing Westmorland, a man who once told an admirable but rather too communicative and agonizing homosexual MP: 'Let me tell you something I don't usually talk about. Can you keep a secret?' 'Yes Michael. Please tell me.' 'I don't believe in God, never have done, no point in it, lot of nonsense got up by the clergy. But I don't go on about it.' For a long time into the Thatcher period Jopling, along with his close friend and neighbour William Whitelaw had a three-quarter hold on the drift and style of government. The whips have always dominated junior appointments – talent scouts armed with a blackball – 'not wise, Prime Minister, too much of this,' followed by a mime involving the elbow or some other part of the body. And these two, the Cumberland and Westmorland Militia representing Country Toryism, with on Whitelaw's part at least a good deal of cautious soft-line good humour, were particularly formidable. They were kin, both of them to the generation, style and class of David Renton.

That authority would wane, but for now in the House Major entered, it mattered a great deal. As the Prime Minister was to say to a friend grumbling about the gloomy unencouraging presence of Patrick Jenkin. 'Yes I *know*, but who is there?' Factions existed with a vengeance, but grooming and seniority during the Heath years had left a bloc of established shadow ministers hard to keep from taking corporeal shape in their limousines, men who by no means belonged to Mrs Thatcher's personal camp or shared her views (views a jolly sight more tentatively advanced in those days). Even the intake were, from her point of view, a sorry lot, far too liberal and a selection largely influenced by a Heathian Central Office.

The first of that intake to get a job was John Patten, charming, stylish but systematically non-ideological, still oddly both there and not much further as perpetual Minister of State in 1991. The thought crossed certain minds that he owed advancement to being not-Chris Patten. The Thatcher runners Lilley, Portillo, Francis Maude were not yet in the House, the available right amounted to Keith Joseph, much mocked but actually the humane variant of Thatcherism, Biffen, sound on economics but subsequently pricked for death following his disinclination to outlaw a trade union, Geoffrey Howe, right wing only on a narrow reading but never quite sound and never truly trusted, Lawson, too junior, and Tebbit, an incomer representing rough trade and the Essex workers. Certain Thatcher henchmen from the days of the anti-Heath *putsch* were thought unsuitable for any kind of ministerial employment. Strangely the most singleminded, sacramental, crawling to the cross, treble dyed, eight-ply cradle Thatcherist was George Gardiner, neither incompetent nor ill-educated whose reward came in the Thatcher resignation honours, a knighthood!

For the ambitious, a favoured route, something much more Tory than Labour in practice was the dining club. The Burke which admits journalists doesn't count, but the Lollards serves the hesitant left, the No Turning Back group (founded after 1983) the black Neapolitan right, and the Blue Chip, a gathering which annoys non-members as cliquish. The Blue Chip does however attract more than the average grouping of people with intellect, presence, application and general aura of future high office. At first Major was one of an unincorporated circle of people who liked one another, might dine together, but not in club form. There was Chris Patten and John Lee; Matthew Parris, Keith Wickenden and Don Thompson are mentioned and Major with them. Major had earlier joined the Guy Fawkes, which is best seen as a rather nice gathering of middling guys. To Major's admirers as well as his detractors, it seems apt.

But he would on the urgent suggestion of Tristan Garel-Jones, that clever one-off original and long-term senior whip, eventually become a member of the Blue Chip, as a result of the impression he was creating as a whip after 1983. Chris Patten insists that the Club is not the ideological gathering or socially homogeneous group it is sometimes called. He cites the presence of himself and Robert Atkins, a great Major friend, as proof of social mix along with Lord Cranborne and Ancram. Major was a regular attender. Patten recalls the club as fun but willing to argue fervently. John, whom he liked, he found more fiscally Conservative, more careful with public money than himself.

Oddly in the light of this slow progress into the golden places, Major was very early indeed the beneficiary of a stupendous piece of long-shot prophecy. Robin Oakley, now political editor of *The Times*, was at that time working for James Goldsmith's magazine *Now*. It was glossy, bright and fashionable, it came out too early for key story collection date, but it paid journalists proper money setting an excellent fashion and shamed many people to do likewise. Very soon after the election Oakley, bought from a national for hair-starting money, justified the fee with a piece about 'The New boys', which said that consensus among the intake about themselves was that the one man among them with the makings of a Prime Minister was John Major. Mr Oakley's case rests.

From the early period of Major's career as an MP his junior colleague, the likeable Gerald Howarth, tells an instructive story. Howarth had for a while been a colleague of Major's at Standard Charter Bank and had political ambitions of his own. When he called on Major at the House, he showed the established Member his draft application for the seat of Cannock and Burntwood. Major was called away from the pleasures of the terrace to a committee meeting. He asked Howarth to linger, and committee being notoriously a place where government MPs vote and stay quiet, returned to Howarth with a heavily re-written text, to which Howarth faithfully stuck. The member for Cannock and Burntwood is fervently appreciative. The men were friendly but not especially close friends nor political allies; Howarth being firmly on the party's right, their tie was simply that of having worked for the same company. But the help was at once forthcoming and in Howarth's view was probably decisively helpful.

At six minutes past seven on Wednesday 13 June 1979 the member for Huntingdon made his maiden speech. Like all maiden speeches it was heard in polite silence. Like all maiden speeches it said something nice about the constitutency and something nice about the previous member. Unlike all maiden speeches it received no commendation about its charm, flair and intimations of a splendid future from the next speaker. Major was followed by the new MP for Bishop Auckland, Derek Foster, now Labour's ineffective Chief Whip. Foster as a new arrival himself could hardly praise another incomer, and the speaker after him, the aged Dr Glyn confined himelf to civilities about Foster. It has not actually mattered.

It is, Major said, twenty-three years since he first sat in the Gallery and heard the 1956 budget debate (he would have been almost thirteen). He had hoped then to take part in debates but didn't realize how long he would have to wait (he was now all of thirty-six). He was proud of the Cromwell association with the town, though expecting to make less trouble for the Speaker, and he liked the local habit of re-electing its members, quoting the eighteenth-century Huntingdon voter who had said, 'Of course we re-elect the member, how else could we be rid of him six months at a time.'

He turned to the budget, observing that it would set a pattern for budgets for that period of government. Four things were required by the public of government, to cut taxes, curb inflation, create new jobs and as far as possible maintain full employment. Public opinion might *require* all four, with the best will, they couldn't be achieved at the same time. The first requirements were two of them: cutting taxes and fighting inflation.

The success of the budget would turn on the degree of resolution to control public expenditure. There would be pressures to break with the cash limits the Government had set. Indeed Mr McGahey of the NUM had just said that conditions were such as to enable the unions to compel the defeat of the Government within eighteen months. Backing away from cash limits would shift the economy off course so he was happy to have heard the Chief Secretary (John Biffen) reiterate a commitment to spending cuts and to restraining the level of expenditure substantially. There would be a certain amount of uproar. It was never popular to cut services.

Public expenditure cuts were acceptable if they were seen to be fair. He was prepared to support a cut in the rate support grant providing that the frugal were not penalized to the advantage of the high spending.

All of this was orthodox, uncontroversial Tory stuff if lucid and terse. He then made a point which reminds us of the huge subterranean changes already taking place in the once rural seat he represented and the odd geminal relationship between his old workplace, Lambeth, and his new home, Huntingdon.

Problems had arisen in Cambridgeshire because of the distribution of the total Rate Support Grant. Cambridgeshire and Huntingdonshire had the most rapidly increasing population of any part of the UK. In Peterborough, St Ives and St Neots the councils had encouraged growth and the acceptance of large overspill from the inner cities, having done that they had found no amendment in the way RSG was distributed. They now received forty per cent of the needs element going to inner city areas. Having spent a great part

Tom and Kitty Major.

Tom Major (centre) with his concert party 'Special Edition' in the early twenties.

Rutlish School cricket team – Major, the slow bowler, standing third from left.

John and Norma with their children Elizabeth and James in the late seventies.

John and Norma on their wedding day, 3 October 1970.

Norma Major with Dame Joan Sutherland.

Victorious after the 1983 elections.

John Major opens the 'Dog and Bone' in Huntingdon, 1989. Left to right: Alan Fox (manager), Susan Fox, John Major, Andrew Ramsay (owner) and Lesley Ramsay.

Canvassing with Sir Fred Catherwood for the 1989 European elections.

With Kenneth Baker and Mike Bloomfield (Constituency Chairman) outside the Huntingdon Conservative Association.

John and Norma Major at Hinchingbrooke Hospital, 1989.

With President George Bush at the Oval Office in 1989.

With William Hague outside 18 Gayfere Street during the leadership campaign, 1990.

Alan Duncan and William Hague at Gayfere Street.

Left to right: Robert Jones, Robert Hughes, Norma Major, John Major, Andrew Mitchell and Terence Higgins.

At home at Great Stukeley.

Visiting the British troops in the Gulf.

of his youth in Brixton Major accepted that there were great problems in such inner city areas, but he trusted the government would look at the maldistribution of the needs element.

Huntingdon didn't need replacement jobs, it needed new jobs since the work had not kept up with the population growth. He was grateful for the tax incentive, offered by Howe and thought they would help create jobs. He called for mitigation of capital transfer tax. Perhaps land should be taxed on its earning capacity and not on the inflated capital value. He welcomed certain social elements in the budget, like the cash increase in the retirement pension. He approved the end of dividend control as it affected savings. However, pensioners could not and did not understand how tax changes could be back-dated to the beginning of the year but retirement pension increases could not. Sophisticated argument might be advanced but would not be understood or accepted. They could surely be paid in November and back-dated to April. Towards the end of his speech Major remarked on the customary absence of interruption, knowing that it wasn't required for the future and wouldn't be given. Having started in Brixton and Camden (the St Pancras seat) he was used to heckling and perhaps really rather preferred it.

His question on 20 June 1979 to the Foreign Office (answered by Sir Ian Gilmour) has a melancholy irony to it. He asked about the recent meeting of what was then the nine states of Europe about political consultation. Sir Ian replied with reference to inadmissibility of acquiring territory by force, the need for Israel to end the territorial occupation, maintained since 1967, respect for sovereignty, territorial integrity and of every state and legitimate right of the Palestinians including their right to a homeland. It sounds familiar.

He was to come back more than once to the question of Urbs in Rus, the special needs of Cambridgeshire because of the migration of population from London to that area, especially to Peterborough new town. He was speaking at a time when old notions of towns needy, country opulent, carried some plausibility at least as rhetoric. But he had learned early as candidate and MP that great bits of Lambeth and places like it had followed to the rim of the fens as the drift to the city of the nineteenth century was put into reverse.

In Huntingdon and St Neots they had huge overspill estates of people fleeing London. They fled for a variety of reasons including, he added partisanly, the policies of inner city Labour authorities. Yet here were Labour Members – he cited a speech just made by John Fraser (Norwood), a pillar of South London Labour politics – brushing aside the needs of the comfortable rural areas.

He was, said Major of himself, an urban creature brought up in South London. He had his own experience of living in 'some of the less salubrious parts of south London.' The problem of Cambridge-shire was that it was accommodating spilt south London without getting enough government money to see it through. When he had been Chairman of Housing briefly in Lambeth, one measure he had been happy to take part in was the establishment of special linkage between that borough and Peterborough new town so that people could move out of appalling conditions into decent estates in the Peterborough area, some of them actually in Huntingdonshire. But the reward for areas outside London for helping had been 'a continuing diminution of funds available.'

Politics being politics he could not resist a quick lunge at certain tempting nonsenses paid for out of the rates by certain left-wing borough authorities. Lambeth and other boroughs were adding to their own problems. He would deal with Lambeth (and perhaps with Camden) he added menacingly if he were pressed to do so. These two were recognized to a substantial degree as spendthrift authorities. They had heavy social problems, they spent money on them; that was understood. But they also went in for a large amount of gratuitous and unnecessary expenditure. An example was the special newspaper produced in Lambeth and distributed to every house in the borough asking people to join a march to protest against the cuts. Whatever the cost, the money might have been better spent on social problems.

Later in the same speech he moved into new territory, the sort from which angels refrain from hurrying into – Rates. He hoped that at some stage we would 'find a better system to finance local government than the rates.' However Major was not about to call for a poll tax or indeed precisely anything. His heart went out, he said, to Tom King then the understrapping Minister at the Environment looking after local goverment whenever anyone suggested that the rating system should immediately be reformed whole-sale.

Anomalies were recognized, however he hoped Mr King would take good time to consider these. When he then brought forward proposals they would be more likely to be right than wrong. (It was about this time, on the evidence of Tom King's then boss Michael Heseltine, that the notion of a Poll Tax was being thrown out in the course of a morning while ministers fell about laughing.) Major went on to mock Labour lightly on the question of rates revaluation: somehow whenever they were in office they had always managed not to have one, they had been good at postponing it. This is historically true but in the light of subsequent events it makes Labour look surprisingly smart. It was to be a later attempt by George Younger at rate revaluation in Scotland which suddenly faced every draper in Montrose and every fishmonger in Dun-fermline with quintrupled bills which first inspired another Scot, Douglas Mason, to offer, and the Prime Minister and Nicholas Ridley, uneasily followed by the Scottish Secretary, to accept, an alternative scheme to be begun in Scotland, one which would solve rate revaluation for all of us!

Devotion to Huntingdon's need for friendly treatment over the Rate Support Grant was to involve the new man in all the heckling he could ask for, one of those strange irrational spats of rage, not quite peculiar to the House of Commons but very familiar there. He made very similar points in an intervention (and taking a side swipe at 'the smug and complacent stand' of Roy Hattersley). But another intervention in the speech of a London Labour member caused him to be mugged – no other word will do – by the intervenee, Ron Brown (the MP for Hackney and Shoreditch, brother of George, no relation to Screaming Ron Brown of Leith and normally a quiet soothing fellow).

It was no use honourable members saying 'No', Council housing had been cut back deliberately. People were then forced to take short-hold tenancies otherwise there was no point in the exercise. Major rose, Brown refused to give way.

When Major had been Chairman of a London borough housing committee he had been heard demanding more money for London. Now he had the effrontery to demand more money for Cambridgeshire. The honourable gentleman was purely dishonest and he knew it. Major got up. Brown continued.

Cambridgeshire might need more money but it did not lie in Major's mouth to speak about it in that way. He found it absolutely nauseating that he should make that kind of intervention. Major asked him to give way. 'No,' said Ron. Major got up again. The honourable Gentleman, went on Brown, had heard him make a challenge before and had done the very same thing. He should have made his remarks in the context of London. London needed the money and he knew it. He might argue on behalf of Cambridge-shire, but he should not put forward an argument so different from the one he used when he had a London responsibility. He should sit back and listen to this speech, if so he would be a wiser man.

There were more fruitless gettings up by Major, more lofty and condescending wavings down by Brown who advised him to sit back and take a little time to consider whether the way he was going on did him any credit. He had, said Ron in his best avuncular voice, been friendly towards the honourable member but the more he saw him doing that kind of thing the more nauseating he found it. He hoped he would take his advice and sit still. If called he could make any points he wished but he would do himself a favour if he would give his tongue a rest and take a rest from doing what he so often did.

Not yet overwhelmed by this tide of improbable allegation and head-patting patronage, Major stopped trying to intervene and turned instead to the deputy-speaker with a point of order. This was a good move. Points of Order are invariably taken, interventions rest with the grace of the current orator. But it is amazing what you can say under the broad canopy of Order.

'On a point of order,' said Major, 'the honourable gentleman's advice was unsought and unwanted.' Perhaps, he hinted, he might endeavour to catch his eye in a few minutes to answer the totally dishonest and unscrupulous remarks made. That, said Jack Weath-erill, was not a point of Order, it was a declaration of intent.

Ron Brown, having exhausted his contempt, continued with the main part of his speech but concluded by saying that though his part of London was not a supplicant, it would be happy if it faced only those problems confronted by the honourable member for Huntingdonshire.

The ploy through points of order worked and Major was called. His response tells us a good deal about the man in his entirety. There is no rage or pique, no desire to embellish the scene already made. It is cool and rational and the outcome was to Commons regulars very nigh sensational.

The honourable gentleman had remembered correctly that when he was Chairman of Housing in Lambeth in the mid sixties ('69–71 actually, the mid-sixties mark Major getting the vote), he was greatly concerned about housing problems of Lambeth. He had done everything that he could to attract to the area the resources the area needed. Would Mr Brown please reflect on the fact that one of the schemes of Major and his colleagues had been to set up an exchange scheme by which many people living in poor conditions in Lambeth were able to migrate to Cambridgeshire specifically to the new town of Peterborough. It had provided a startling success. Part of that new town to which people had moved now fell into his constituency of Huntingdonshire. Surely Mr Brown would acquit him of the unparliamentary allegation of dishonesty.

He had repeatedly made the point about the RSG allocation. There had been a dramatic move of population particularly to the outskirts of the shire counties outside London. Cambridgeshire, for which he had pleaded and intervened, had the swiftest growing population of any county in Britain, his constituency (no longer a county in any but parliamentary terms) was its swiftest growing component part. The electoral register showed it as more than doubling since the general election of 1966. The net loss to Cambridgeshire from allocation of RSG over the previous four years had been twenty million pounds plus. He was not asking for special treatment because he understood, remembered and recognized the problems existing in London, including those of Hackney and Shoreditch.

Cambridgeshire with the best will in the world had endeavoured to help London. They had accepted the people from London from their area with an open heart and a ready will. However the people should not be asked to accept a population and then be denied the wherewithall to deal with it. If that continued they and the other developing areas like Bracknell would say, 'No more will we endeavour to help solve the problems of inner London.' Would Mr Brown accept that he, Major, had constantly attempted to get not preferential treatment for the county he represented but a fair allocation of Rate Support Grant, that and no more?

What follows is to connoisseurs of parliamentary rough house pure sensation. Ron Brown said that he unreservedly withdrew the abuse that he had poured upon the honourable gentleman's head. He had thought Mr Major was saying that London had more than was sufficient and that it should now be transferred to places like Cambridgeshire. He now understood that Major was saying there should be a fairer balance of the needs of London and those of Cambridgeshire. Therefore he withdrew any imputation that he was arguing 'less for London, more for Cambridgeshire.'

Major got up and said, 'I am most grateful to the Honourable Gentleman.'

This handling of a hot-headed, well-meaning opponent who had grasped the wrong end of a complicated stick is kin with the reputation Major would make as Whip, Social Security Minister and Chief Secretary – a name for conciliation through reasoned argument, for moving people poised for conflict into acceptance that their case was carefully understood and gently if denyingly answered. Spats between backbenchers in the Commons are not important in themselves but the resolution of this one is an insight into a crucial quality of the present Prime Minister, the low temperature physics of Major's political personality.

However he was entirely capable of sharp, well-phrased and combative language. There is nothing grey about this lunge at Roy Hattersley. 'Bluster, dubious antics and phoney logic,' he did not believe that he could fashion a phrase as adequately identifying the kind of performance one had come to expect from the honourable gentleman. His speech was marked by a dubious use of logic and a smug assertion that everything done by the Minister (Heseltine – Environment) was done for the worst of all possible reasons to create the worst of all possible problems.

But Major shifts gear quickly from the *ad hominem* poke in the eye with a burnt stick to a calm argument about fact, before shifting it again to make with a straight face a virtuoso appeal for less personal abuse among MPs! First the factual argument: was it alleged that the cutting of the capital allocation for housing was meant as an attempt to cut out council housing altogether? If so they were bound to ask Labour, if that was their motive when they halved the capital allocation for housing in the two or three years before the last election. If it was their motive, would they admit it, if not how could they say that it was this Minister's motive?

The plea for charity followed. This was the sort of malicious and irrelevant remark which deliberately divided the House far more than necessary. He did not wish to sound pompous if he said that, looking at the House from the outside, that was the kind of extravagant remark which devalued its prestige among those who elected them.

However, having done the pious bit he turned deftly back to smack Hattersley's head. That politician had said 'all the pat, socially conscious phrases he could produce. If there was a problem we could be certain that the honourable gentleman knew about it, has an opinion about it and that that opinion would be on the side of the angels of the day. He would embrace any folly and any absurdity if he saw a temporary advantage to himself in doing so.'

This was good crisp unmaliciously partisan politics (odd how one can bear the belabouring of Mr Hattersley with so much fortitude), and he went on to develop a conscientious Conservative argument against Hattersley's uneconomic hopes that a particular wage claim would breach the six per cent hoped for (against the pure spirit of monetarism) by the Government. But he added something thoroughly at odds with the Thatcher norm. He understood the nature of the crisis and the part which oil prices had played in it, he understood that reductions in capital allocations for housing had proved necessary thus far. *However if the Treasury came back looking for more, he could assure his friend the Secretary of State that he would have a far greater measure of backbench support than he may realize if he should tell the Chancellor of the Exchequer that there is no capacity for further capital cuts in the Housing investment programme in the foreseeable future. Housing had born its share of cuts and in capital terms a substantial share. There should be no more.* The Italics are mine but they stress a vein in Major very much his own and out of the fashion for rising young men in the Conservative Party. This is Harry Simpson speaking, the man who educated his young men about the replacement of slums. It is emphatically not Milton Friedman.

He was however able in a defence of shorthold tenure, a Conservative favourite of the time, to resume the agreeable business of clumping Labour for narrow impercipience. This involved the particular pleasure of slapping down David Winnick who had asked if Major could not understand that there had to be security of tenure. There was, said Major shortly, even less security of tenure in being homeless than in having only twelve months security with the possibility of renewal. Gerald Kaufman, then shadowing, had said Labour would repeal the provision as soon as they had the chance. They chose not to wait to see if the scheme worked. They had made up their minds, consequently the scheme was crucified before it had a chance to operate. Hattersley had expressed opposition to shorthold before the Standing committee had even met to discuss it. What an open mind this portrayed to those who were homeless and might have benefited from it.

The impression of Major from reading his speeches, and most backbenchers speak between six and nine to audiences in single figures, of whom only one (the recording angel of a note-taking whip) is really listening, is of a sensible pragmatic Tory, not a monetarist or a Thatcherite nor a rebel in the mould of Cyril Townsend or more tentatively his friend George Young. He is not a voluminous speaker either, in the index of Hansard his name is more thinly scattered than any number of much lesser men. The central judgment remains true that he expresses no unneccesary opinions. But he speaks well enough, in a cool, dry ironical way not in the least grey but for now happy enough with the shadows.

7

Junior Office

When, after the elections of 1983, Major was given his first job, as a junior whip, he entered a subtle company, a working élite which one whip, Archie Hamilton, cheerfully calls the Broederbond.

The British whip system, controlling parties with a regimental tradition of solidarity, is unlike anything known in America where the electoral district is king and the party system a loose association of consent. But the Tory whips office is very different in turn from that of the Labour Party. Labour members historically have more often run scared of their constituency General Management Committees. This happens much less in this decade than the last, though the experience of Frank Field, outstanding specialist in the social services, deferred to by Tory ministers like Tony Newton as probably knowing as much about the subject as the department, but still the subject of a Merseyside lynch mob, is a very nasty reminder.

But broadly, the authority of Labour whips in the House of Commons is lighter than for Conservatives. It is accepted that in a radical party people will want to rebel and if they are rebelling from the Left invariably they have constituency support. In a party where major shadow office is won by internal election, the whips have limited inducements to compliance. Few things are more gaily spurned than shadow junior office, that carrot's ghost. Labour Whips have fitful authority relying on a heavy manner, appeals to loyalty and outspread hands. Broadly, that party plays to almost

American rules except that the MP defers to his local organization rather than his mere voters.

The saddest comment on Labour whips relates not to great issues but to the idle, non-operative nature of a group of low-grade MPs contemptuously known as the dossers, contributing little except a bloc of votes at the annual whips' election and giving support to the most complacent, least dynamic claimant on that post, a guarantee that committee and chamber work will never be done with the vigour and trouble both require. Thin attendances at key debates – twenty on average even on opposition days against seventy-five plus for government supporters – and the absence of regular harrying campaigns based on some preparatory work in committee are direct consequences of this state of affairs.

Tory constituencies are capable of extreme opinions and much unpleasantness (witness the response to those openly involved against Mrs Thatcher last autumn). But ignorance of politics and broad support for The Party (Soviet style), some social aspiration or resentment, as in Major's own selection against the Marquess of Douro, essentially keep associations quiescent. Only latterly with the rise of right-wing cells, has there been much activity that could be called ideological.

Accordingly, the Conservative whips inherit a position of strength nowhere equalled in the English speaking world. Deferential associations, a parliamentary party about eighty three per cent ambitious if only for budgerigar-seed, persuasive authority over all junior appointments which, since in Britain they are the pre-condition of higher appointments, means guardianship of the ladder to the top, a shameless traffic in honours with knighthood as the parliamentary party's long-service medal, also a brisk bourse in committee places and free trips – powers of let or stay over who gets tickets for fact-finding missions, in Rio or Bangkok – who punitively will investigate Belgian social services – list the means to hand and we are talking power.

The Conservative whips enjoy in their small but influential kingdom, a power which, compared with the lot of a middle eastern despot, armed only with life and death and control of the press and television, might fall short in crude overkill, but which in its finely nuanced way suffices.

Something else, the Labour Whips Office is rarely an avenue to other ministerial office. People either oblige by standing in there for a short unwelcome time before getting out to preferred slots or back to the backbenches, or alternatively, they remain as long-service, non-commissioned officers. The quality of Labour whips is low and without further aspiration; that of Tory whips broadly very good, and ever since Edward Heath emerged from the Chief Whip's office on to a major career curve in the early sixties, a steady flow of whips has irrigated ministerial jobs. Of John Major's rough contemporaries, Ian Lang is Secretary of State for Scotland, Archie Hamilton is Minister of State for Defence, Tristan Garel-Jones is Minister of State at the Foreign Office, John Wakeham having been Leader of the House is Energy Secretary, David Hunt is Welsh Secretary, Alistair Goodlad is Deputy Chief Whip and Richard Ryder as Chief Whip is the Prime Minister's Prime Minister, his single most important appointment.

There are of course career whips in every batch not expecting, or at any rate not getting, ministerial jobs. At this time younger whips talked affectionately about 'the colonels': Carol Mather and Bob Boscawen, solid fatherly figures to offset the beating of hawks' wings. There is often the lowering figure of an enforcer, a coercive heavy not intended for high office but good at a little, highly controlled bullying where subtlety seems inappropriate. But this sort of Oddjob figure, currently the unengaging David Lightbown, is a marginal resource.

The central truth about Tory whips office is that it has great quantities of power, extensive sophistication, patronage, direct responsibility for the enactment of legislation and it acts as a liaison channel between government and backbenches. Whips are intended not just to sell the bosses' wishes to the rank and file, they must tell the people in the Great House about the mood of the peasantry. Early reports of muttering in the alehouse can avert an outburst of rick burning. Governments can, if they wish, force through all manner of legislation – I have often contemplated the close but sufficient majority with perhaps thirty-five abstentions, available on the Innocents (Massacre of, Number One) Bill. But if they have any sense they listen to reports gathered in tearoom, bar, Ways and Means corridor and general chat and gossip. If Mrs Thatcher had heeded what whips told her about the parliamentary Conservative Party's view of the poll tax this would be the biography of the Chancellor of the Exchequer.

The whips who have a lively understanding of the powers they have accumulated, do not lightly make new admissions. Every nominee has his name canvassed with the established whips and a single dissenter has a veto. When John Major's name went round it was universally acceptable. 'I will not kid you,' says one advocate of Major already established there, 'that I was not pushing at an open door. People like that,' he added, 'don't need special protection, they are just fucking good.' He was entered a little later for the Blue Chip Club on a piece of advocacy from Tristan Garel-Jones which in his words said, 'I don't know if you know it but there is this chap in the Whips Office with me. And he is top bloody flight.'

Indeed enthusiasm from some quarters outran that of the then Chief Whip, Michael Jopling. Asked about the new man, one replied keenly, 'Oh absolutely, I think this man has ministerial potential.' Jopling himself about to leave for a tour of duty in the Ministry of Agriculture protesting wanly against the Common Agricultural Policy budget, gave one of his dour looks and said, 'Oh do you think so? I wouldn't go that far.' An interesting refusal to buy at the bottom of a rather good market.

Every new whip is given two assignations: to a part of the country and to a department. The first, which is usually his own region, will stick but the Department is shifted annually. 'It isn't our intention,' says John Wakeham, Major's boss for all but his first two months, 'that a chap hired to be our man in the ministry becomes the ministry's man in the whips office.' So as it were, a whip may start as North Western whip coupling with education but moving on the next year to trade and industry or occasionally combining a couple of lighter departments. He is also required to be expert on the raw material of politics, the politicians. The view of that responsibility which follows is that of an experienced and highly regarded former whip.

A good whip knows each man's ambitions, strengths, weaknesses, what they have done and would like to do. There is an old whips' game – if a whip sees two politicians talking in the lobby he likes to think he can guess what they are talking about.

'The other half of his job relates to legislation; the whip being responsible for seeing that a bill is delivered on time. For this he has a surprising amount of authority. This extends to the power to tell his minister to shut up and get on with it. The whip not the minister should do the deals with the opposition about the timetable (these really are the 'usual channels'), he does the deals on which bits of the bill may be dropped or not and advising the minister on the views of parliamentary colleagues about whether he can get a given section through.

'Some whips may be better at different aspects of their job but ideally they should be able to do it all. It is not a whip's job to get in the way but to make sure that he watches what happens and sees it doesn't go wrong. When a whip starts voicing his own opinion, butting in, taking over a minister's role it won't work. Whips are there to make something work even better than it would otherwise and to guard against trouble. The best of the whips know the detail of the legislation, you can get by without it but you are not a good whip. The man who knows the detail can spot trouble coming. The job is to say, "We are now on Clause 5, when we get to Clause 15 we are going to get into trouble because X is a specialist on Outer Space and the clause is designed to make him amend it." You must square him before he puts an amendment down because when he does he will be hooked on it and so will you be. He can't get off without losing face. So think ahead, determine what it is and stop him doing something unhelpful to you both.

'You can't plan like that without knowing both members and their qualities and the details of a given bill.'

This multiple requirement of knowing the people intimately for their resources and the issues for the explosive potential of otherwise boring-looking detail seems to John Major himself to give the Whips Office qualities which other people see in Sandhurst or Manchester Grammar School.

He observes the talents late of that office now rising elsewhere – Michael Portillo and David Hunt, nominally from opposite ends of the Tory Party, though one wouldn't think it to hear Hunt loyally promoting the Poll Tax. He also speaks warmly of David Maclean, a younger, more junior politician and by no means every onlooker's favourite, all were proof of the excellence of the whips office. Rarely does a graduate of that academy in the Prime Minister's view fail outside it, though of course he concedes the excellence of many who have not been through that school, giving the two Pattens as examples.

It was in his ministerial secondings that arguably Major began to make his reputation. By no means did most whips, even conscientious ones, think it right to become too involved in the minutiae of departmental legislative problems. It would be a little like captains in the pioneer corps worrying too much about geology. One whip put it plainly: 'Most of us would come bumbling back from the department having had a general gossip about politics with ministers but not really much wiser. But John would come back with everything tied up. He would say, "well they've got this piece of legislation which is mostly alright, but over *this* point they have anxieties and over *that* one the Opposition should score heavily." '

He was performing the role of a specifically political whip, telling his own office where the snags would come, what might provoke backbench unease or even rebellion. If it were possible after the First World War to speak well of a staff officer, he was functioning as a high-class staff officer. 'At the same time,' one is told, 'there was nothing smug or swotlike in this performance. He was doing a lot of homework and being enormously useful to the office but he wasn't getting pleased with himself. The other thing about John is that despite humble origins, unlike Smiggs and Flipper,' (he named two ministers), 'he doesn't have a chip on his shoulder.' He was also to win a reputation with backbenchers which would do him no harm in November 1990. He is widely reported for scrupulous regard for confidences, not reporting views given to him unless he actually said, 'I have to tell that to the Chief Whip.' He was able in fact to distinguish briefing from gossip or snooping.

He was also respected for himself, performing what he asked. If there was a late vote to which he had guided his East Anglian fiefdom specifically, he did not take advantage of a whip's rota of attendance to be gone early himself. He would be on the front bench waiting for the bell just like the people he had rounded up. A whip pointed out that the whips office does discuss things. It is mooted that one colleague intends to canvass opinion on a contentious issue. 'So in those days Wakeham, Chief Whip at the time, would send it round the table. John, when it reached him, would say, "Well, Chief, I think the issue for the party on this one is *dadadada*. And I think, if he is going to carry it out the way he should, he should do it like this *dadadada*."' End of discussion.

'Also,' this witness added, looking forward to the wider career, 'an underrated virtue, he knows how to do nothing. Too many people bubble with ideas all the time. Do this. Do that. John thinks through very hard, does it and then allows it to roll.'

A final thought on the character of the Prime Minister came from another source. 'There is a certain internal hardness and toughness. There are very few people who've seen this. I've seen it but I don't intend to repeat details of the occasions when I have seen it. Suffice it to say that if John Major thought someone was incompetent he would deal with them with total toughness, not with any ill-feeling but with rock-like toughness. I've got no doubts that this is a tough guy.'

There was, however, to be a mighty obstacle and problem for Major personally, one which for all his sedulousness, he had not foreseen. It was the custom of the whips to give a dinner party for the Prime Minister, 'a really pleasant occasion,' said one whip fond of Thatcher. 'She could kick her shoes off and we would bat things back and forth but no heavy argument. It emphatically wasn't meant to be an occasion for earnest debate.' Mrs Thatcher having enjoyed herself and entertaining warm feelings for the whips decided to return the compliment and give her own dinner party for them. 'Unfortunately,' says this witness, a horrified participant in the evening, 'she wanted to bring in the Lords whips. Frankly,' he adds, 'they don't count, only semi-political, don't know the rules. It was a bad case of diluting the Mafia. They raised some winge or other. That started *her* up and she wanted an answer from us. However, Major most uncharacteristically started getting ratty and he argued the case very strongly. She of course simply tore into him, she does have this way of going for the messenger. He came right back and said, "Prime Minister, you asked me to report and give you an account. That is what I am doing." To call this embarrassing is a hell of an understatement. John just got more and more angry looking almost ready to walk out. The rest of us just sat there squirming'.

'There was,' adds this informant, 'a strong feeling that perhaps, as far as his career went, he had shot his bolt. But Denis (Thatcher) was there – by the way Denis shouldn't have had a baronetcy, he should have had a Dukedom. He's completely sensible and he has a heart of gold – and Denis said to him, "Don't worry my boy. The old girl does fly off the handle at times and gets like this."' ' There is a very strong inference, which no one can absolutely verify, that the present Prime Minister may in the days after that turbulent night have owed his survival on any sort of career path to the soothing, worldly good sense of the last Prime Minister's husband. In which case a hereditary title to please a loving husband and father must have been recommended with some fervour.

This is the rough account of an onlooking whip. A rather fuller and more detailed history of these events is even more vivid.

Although the party was Mrs Thatcher's and she acted as hostess, the chair was taken by the acting Chief Whip, John Cope, a soft-voiced low-ego Yorkshireman subsequently (and wrongly) denied the job of chief for having given Mrs Thatcher too much bad news dressed in insufficient tact, something which in the light of this night's events is ironical. Cope turned to Major as Treasury whip for a résumé of party opinion in the Commons. Major said that though *he* thought economic policy was right, there was a volume of unease. He then listed a series of issues which had caused mutter-ing, the low scale of capital investment prominent among them. He was heard in silence from all present and at the end of his summary Mrs Thatcher said, 'You astound me,' and launched a great attack, addressed to Major but concerned with what he had said. He replied, 'Hang on a minute. I'm telling you what the *party* thinks. That's *what* they think whether it's agreeable or not.' There was then 'another great attack' to which he responded again, and finally a fourth time. The table stayed rigid with anxious silence, except for Carol Mather. Now Carol Mather and his great friend Bob Boscawen were known, entirely affectionately, as 'the Colonels'. They were senior whips of a more old-fashioned kind who did not aspire to ministerial office after service as whips. They were also older men, but ones who built a great deal of stability and strength into the whips office. Both, being ex-soldiers, were strong on old-fashioned loyalty. Carol Mather trying to support John Major, was given short shrift by Mrs Thatcher. Bob Boscawen wasn't going to have his friend treated like that so *he* weighed in on the side of the young man.

The fight only broke up and good humour was only restored when one particularly ineffable lordship, a whip, observed, 'Prime Minister, you're so right': 'What am I right about?' 'I've forgotten,' said the peer, 'but you're so right.' This at least broke the tension.

The indulgent view which Major himself takes is that Mrs Thatcher was enjoying herself, having one of those battling-Maggie arguments which she required to win. Others will see only the reflexive bullying which recurringly and across cabinets created so much fear in grown men.

There was quite a view afterwards that this was the end of Major's career, that he had been too blunt, had not given the necessary inch. He wasn't certain himself and speaking to his wife said that he had had no alternative but to speak as he did, but 'she should know that there had been the most colossal row.' John Wakeham insisted afterwards that he should not worry and Denis Thatcher (about whose presence at the meal itself no one is quite sure) clapped Major on the shoulder saying, 'She'll have enjoyed that.' But it had been a big row which went on and on and he was only a junior whip.

In fact Mrs Thatcher proceeded very quickly to undo his fears. She came next day to sit next to him on the bench and ask his opinion about a routine piece of parliamentary business. She asked in particular about a set of briefing notes. Uncharacteristically, he hadn't seen them and didn't like to say that he hadn't, so he suggested that they needed a bit of work. 'Right,' she said, 'let's go and look at them,' and called a little *ad hoc* meeting in the Whips Office to check them out. In showing this mixture of friendliness and business as usual she was saving Major from days, perhaps weeks, of bust-career anxiety. He believes that she is entirely tolerant of sincere dissent providing it comes from people sharing her premises. His own experience may perhaps rather sustain another view of her that she beats up rivals and peers and is much kinder to junior unexalted people.

He was to have an opportunity in his first post after leaving the whips office – as a junior social security minister – to demonstrate qualities Mrs Thatcher admired. 'That,' says an observer, 'came over pensions. As in the whips office, he had all the details and was perfectly briefed. Most people are attracted by opposites. Here it was a case of the attraction of likes, he has the same elephantine memory she has.' The move was welcome, despite the good opinions won in the whips office, Major was noticed chafing. Just as he had grumbled mildly to Norma about other people getting first jobs ahead of him in the period 1979–83, he was hoping for a shift after two years as a whip. The DHSS was then a single mega-ministry under the melancholy suzerainty of Norman Fowler. Tony Newton, the Minister of State on the Social Security side (who in 1979 had been his regional whip and had early formed a high opinion of him, as a housing specialist and in debate), had specifically suggested Major as a junior colleague. The Department was quite a happy ship in personal terms, but, to vary the metaphor a little, it might be called a happy minefield. Edwina Currie, a good friend, had come horribly unstuck at the health end of operations. An able man lacking grasp of dull detail, Ray Whitney had recently been fatally trapped in the same job, Under Secretary for Social Security, into which Major was moving.

Major himself observes that only a handful of people in the Commons fully understand the labyrinth of social security. Tony Newton, Nick Scott, Frank Field and Margaret Beckett are given as examples of the two dozen or so he thinks qualify. So as he remarks himself, 'In the country of the blind the one-eyed man is king.'

When Major joined, the Department was hard at work at the Fowler reforms, the future social security Act of 1986 – income related benefits, changes in Serps and facilitation of personal pensions. Newton is sincerely enthusiastic about having had Major as a colleague. With so much work, most of it detail, unfussed high competence is at a premium. A relief to Newton was that Major could be left to get on with his allocation of business; another his skill and soothing ways with a quite combative committee. Newton himself now Secretary of State for the independent DSS, also recalls the collegiate and happily co-operative nature of that team.

The only point of contention concerns the predisposition of Norman Fowler to pizzas. In those days the department, now housed in the sweet geometric Gothic nouveau of Richmond House, lived over the underpass at the Elephant (in the unspeakable Alexander Fleming House). Nearby was a pizza house to which it was Fowler's delight to adjourn his Monday morning meeting with colleagues. The local pizzas, says Major, 'were drenched in garlic.' Colleagues would eventually notice how the otherwise convivial, gregarious junior minister had organized a series of items of other business which took him away with sad regularity from Monday lunch with his office friends.

A Parliamentary Under Secretary away from his department is a political carbon speck. Occasionally though he gets a chance to impress, though he is also vulnerable to the put-downs of inadvertence.

Nigel Wicks, Second Secretary at the Treasury, tells two light pleasant anecdotes about Major in his days at the DHSS. The first concerns an encounter with Jack Jones. The former General Secretary of the Transport and General Workers Union has made himself into a formidable lobbyist for the interests of pensioners. Having become one he felt the urge to organize them generally. For some time now he has been leading a posse of old folk on an annual descent upon the Prime Minister. The event brings out the courtly side of both Mrs Thatcher and Mr Jones, but is seen with some trepidation by civil servants since they are generally thrown on the defensive and obliged to justify themselves. The Junior Minister from the DHSS, as it was at this time, might find himself either flustered or aloof in his handling of a distinctly sensitive occasion. Wicks was thus startled to be told on the stairs by a colleague 'Well we've just won that one.' 'How on earth did that happen?' 'There was this parliamentary secretary from Social Security who was extremely well briefed, was extremely courteous and could answer all their questions.' 'Who was it?' 'John Major.' For this reason the episode had not been totally defensive and the Government had gently got some points across.

The second, mildly embarrassing, episode concerns a meeting of cabinet ministers, not a cabinet meeting, to which Major had been asked as a junior to be on hand for certain possible technical issues. Wicks recalls saying, 'Oh stick him in the waiting room.' Half an hour later a messenger came up and said 'Sir. That gentleman, Sir, is still sitting in the waiting room.' Wicks, whose mind Major had slipped, hurried to make apologies at this oversight. 'Major just grinned and said, "Don't worry. It's the job of parliamentary secretaries to wait." '

He had done enough as a junior, even if the Second Secretary had temporarily mislaid him, for his immediate boss, Tony Newton, to feel easy late in 1986 about making the sideways move to run the Ministry of State at health, vacating his own place to Major. The few months Major spent as Minister of State for Social Security are marked by a famous if misty occasion when, himself, suddenly caught up in a whirl of press attention, he brought argument to bear on Mrs Thatcher with resonating effect.

The matter of emergency heating payments, something deriving from a set of free standing regulations, crashed on to Major's desk shortly after he moved up inside the DHSS to become Minister of State for Social Security. 'For a few glorious days,' he says, 'I was the most hated man in Britain.'

The epithet, Mr Coldsnap, was used though it never quite caught on. The payments themselves, baroque in their definition of eligibility in the way of that department and frugal in their general intent, had been fashioned before he moved to that responsibility. But there was a snap not unlike the one in February 1991 of blasting, earlobe-detaching weather of the kind regular enough but always in Britain viewed by the authorities like an extra planetary incursion.

Major recalls constant bombardment over a short time. He gave endless radio and TV interviews, he was asked on the Monday which had been particularly cold, if he had elderly parents (both were of course dead) and his brother Terry also found enquiring voices at the end of his phone. There were masses of headlines: 'I drove up from Huntingdon in the snow,' he says, 'and gave eighteen media interviews in one day. I may be slow but I'm not that slow.'

He set about shifting course. Arguably it was the key moment of his career, one which required the instincts of a whip, recognizing trouble and finding a way out of it. The opposition had been having the time of its life in session for continuous indignation and a line in what about the old folk – not the less effective for the identifiable element of self-service it contained.

Major made his first efforts with the Treasury and found them not so much hostile as edgy – the Treasury, he says, are generally edgy on such occasions but the relevent minister, the Chief Secretary John MacGregor, did not leap to concede. Accordingly Major went up to the only place up, the Prime Minister's office. She was open to persuasion which he believes involved them both going to the window where he remarked how cold it was out there. Mrs Thatcher is, most of the time, a practical politician. Armed with her understanding, he then had no difficulty in exacting all necessary concessions from MacGregor. He was able to make his announcement to the Commons leaving the Opposition with its base of injustice cut from beneath it, orating in mid-air. A bad, over-elaborate and grudging regulation had been hammered into something better if neither simple nor lavish because the relevant minister responded to press and public opinion, took it seriously and won concessions from the top. It was a demonstration of sensible government, but also the first public showing of the skills and resources of this minister. The first articles about Major's big future, the ones which embarrassed him, appeared soon after on the heels of derisive dismissal of Mr Coldsnap.

The vital transition to the Cabinet came after the 1987 election. However meretriciously and with no matter what economic troubles on the stove, the Tories were back, their majority barely dented. Major might hardly have expected promotion. He was after all only nine months into his promotion to Minister of State at Social Security. But there were steady rumours – I was fortunate enough to pick one up myself and print it – that Major was destined for the office of Chief Whip. It would have been a brilliant run for someone in Parliament for only two terms. And in fact we know on uncontradictable assurance that he was indeed slated by the Prime Minister for just this job.

The point is made by a very astute whips office figure that the decision to switch him to the Chief Secretaryship was momentous – for him and for Margaret Thatcher. 'Arguably,' said my informant, 'the Chief Whip is more important than the Chief Secretary – not in the Cabinet indeed, but enormously powerful and influential. But Major as Chief would have saved Margaret Thatcher.' The actual Chief in 1990 was Tim Renton, a perfectly competent and loyal fellow though not experienced in the office before, oddly, coming in as its boss. But having made that personal choice Mrs Thatcher,

I was told, withheld confidence from him – perhaps as a close friend of Sir Geoffrey Howe. Without such confidence the defence of the Prime Minister's back could never be assured.

But, it was pointed out, while Major would have saved Thatcher, being the first-class professional whip he was and commanding her goodwill, he would by November 1990 just about be moving into his first cabinet job, perhaps a good one but not as good as Chancellor and not as good as Prime Minister.

What saved him from this role as a useful but partly sidelined functionary was the insistence of Nigel Lawson, who very late insisted, 'I want this man for Chief Secretary.' After a year looking after the Department of the Environment, Major had been made Treasury whip. This was a fast promotion partly due to merit but due also to the view of the man whose turn it roughly was, Tristan Garel-Jones, a foreign affairs specialist now Minister of State at the FO, that the technical side of the Treasury would leave him feeling uneasy. Major also badly wanted the job and Garel-Jones informed John Cope, deputy chief, that he would prefer not to go.

How good he had been is best expressed in the view attributed to Nigel Lawson on a separate occasion, that he was 'without a doubt the best whip that Nigel had ever seen.' Given Lawson's enormous authority at that time, the architect of victory, someone with whom the Prime Minister was nervous of arguing, who once said in Cabinet, and lived, 'Do be quiet, Margaret,' he was hardly to be refused. The reason for Lawson's esteem turned in part upon the quality of Major's reports to Treasury ministerial meetings of the parliamentary state of play. These reports would take, I was told, perhaps three minutes and be masterpieces of succinct accurate clarity.

This was the move in Major's career which put him in the Cabinet well ahead of schedule even for the very able, and gave him the post commanding extensive, sustained, direct relations with other colleagues. From someone remarkable for outstanding one-to-one relations, it was the best of all chances, the prospect of making a reputation and a spectrum of friends at the same time.

8

Chief Secretary

Major then had been immediately evident to Nigel Lawson as a
talent, even as a new member. 'Evidently,' says the ex-chan-
cellor, 'more mature than most young MPs.' He would have been
offered a job very straight off in 1979 as PPS to the Financial
Secretary to the Treasury, Lawson's first post, but the whips inti-
mated that policy was to keep the new men hungry or at any rate
acquiring experience of not being ministers.

Major was noticed by Lawson as a whip when in 1984 he was
attached to the department as Treasury whip. He followed David
Hunt in this post. Hunt, who rose to the Cabinet (Wales) by way
of interim promotion as deputy chief whip and the gruesome office
of legislative custodian of the Poll Tax, was deemed by the Chancellor to be a very good Treasury whip indeed; John Major was
'quite as good, possibly even better.' The strength and the usefulness
appeared in 'Prayer meetings', little sortings out of problems done
together by Treasury ministers in which the Treasury whip was
asked to report back on the legislature and its problems, difficulties
ahead, and anxieties among the rank and file.

Major was to be admired by the Chancellor for exceptional political talent, for spotting political problems which needed attention,
setting them out clearly without waste of words and getting to the
point. The Treasury would have problems with the back benches
and his rapport with them was exceptional.

Later, after Major had gone to the DHSS, he was kept in touch with the Treasury when he was invited to join the Chancellor's ideas group, one of several assembled by ministers with many co-options to advance ideas for the election manifesto. A cool view of these undertakings is taken by some who saw them as essentially a public relations exercise, an attempt to stroke the hair of backbenchers, PPSs and other riffraff. Major's involvement here was not heavy since ministerial duties kept him pre-occupied, but his suggestions, though not frequent, were all deemed sensible. He had the good will and professional respect of Lawson.

Proof came with the reshuffle following the Conservative return in June 1987 with an only slightly tempered majority. A committee of Thatcher, Lawson and William Whitelaw, with John Wakeham making a late contribution, was giving out and taking away jobs. Thatcher, who had been impressed by Major and had moved him up from bronze to silver (Parliamentary Secretary to Minister of State) in nine months, at the urging of his departmental colleagues, had decided that she wanted Major for Chief Whip.

It is not uncommon for the Chief Whip to be a former Lord Treasurer (senior whip as Major had been), who had gained experience without calamity in a couple of junior or middle-rank ministerial appointments. Apart from the fact that he would be running very fast – two years only out of the office before coming back as Chief – his appointment would, in a telescoped way, have been orthodox. Lawson, however, argued strongly against the appointment. He was losing John MacGregor, a deputy he greatly valued – rightly, for MacGregor is an intelligent, companionable man if not over terse.

The Chief Secretaryship matters enormously; it was important that it should be done well, indeed that it should not be done badly. The contrasting examples of recent Chief Secretaries were something of a two-man morality tale; MacGregor, polite, expert, fully on top of a string of departments and willing to wade through rivers of work, and Peter Rees, according to consensual witnesses, few of these things. Rees is recalled as being uninstructable.

Major had shown with his deft whipping and his handling of the heating allowance affair, the precise mix of hard work and grasp, of political angle and sharp edges not walked into, wanted in a Chief Secretary. The job itself – in the Cabinet and involving the affairs of other departments – ultimately mattered more than the Whips Office in all its glory. As Major himself puts it, 'You know where all the bodies are buried, indeed you buried some of them yourself.'

Thatcher had not been keen on the move, especially she was not keen on having her made-up mind unscrambled for her. But at this time her Chancellor was high in Thatcher's esteem, as had been the case since Lawson had in 1981–3 stacked coal for the future quartermastering of the siege of the NUM and its lovable leader. They got on for this entire five-year period exceptionally well. Though there was a contemporary disfunction which might have warned Lawson. Norman Tebbit, as close to her and perhaps warmer yet in his attachment, had, for no coherent reason except the ambitions of a garrulous adman and a little admired colleague, become distanced from Mrs Thatcher's trust. As another senior minister remarked, she seemed to have a compulsion to quarrel with perfectly loyal, good colleagues. Lawson's turn would come to see her love discandy and all her sweetness poured into another, but at that moment in 1987 he actually *was* unassailable. If he asked firmly enough for Major as his deputy at the Treasury he could have him.

Especially was this true since he had no trouble in answering the question, 'Who would you have for Chief whip?' He offered David Waddington, a whip some years before and since, a tough but widely liked Minister of State, notably at the Home Office (to which in an exalted fashion he would later return). Thatcher hadn't given a thought to Waddington, but she recognized that he was on the right of the party, if not quite of her own ideological kitchen-hob group, and that he would be a clear-minded, unfussed chief. (She should later have had the wit to keep him there!) Accordingly, by a late amendment, John Major delightedly became Chief Secretary and David Waddington, to his pleased surprise, Chief Whip.

At the start of his time as Chief Secretary, Major, also surprised since he had received firm hints about the Whips Office, was to be startled by the sheer volume of work. A Chief Secretary is universal nanny, in the business of saying, 'Don't do that,' to a whole assembly of Georges, but obliged actually to know minutely *why* they shouldn't and to hold up his end with a succession of departmental ministers each of whose civil servants have briefed him on this single narrow front. He would have to give hard expert reasons why money, if witheld, would not cause riots, the deaths of babies in their cots and the resignation of conspicuous numbers of Conservative county councillors. What Ministers must know on a single front, the Chief Secretary needs to master in respect of Education, Defence, Health, Social Security, the Home Office, the Foreign Office, Housing and Local Government, Transport, Scotland, Overseas Aid, Wales and the Universe. In Major's own words, it is like being a whip in spades.

As one of his officials was to point out, it is an exceptionally good training ground for a Prime Minister, not a launch pad but a training ground. There bright politicians actually learned what the running business of a whole government was. Major is very emphatic about its nature. 'The hardest worked job in government, harder than Chancellor,' he says, and one involving attending all Cabinet sub-committees. 'One is a pivot of all discussions in Cabinet sub-committee except for the few the Chancellor does for you and there are precious few of those. You see a lot of the Prime Minister. During an average week you might attend ten meetings of an hour to an hour and a half each under her chairmanship. One was also put into the position of arguing on the same side, since the Prime Minister's view and that of the Treasury tend to coincide.' There might be differences but he had his experience in the job of persuading the Prime Minister to accept some policy moves she had at first resisted.

Major, in his first Cabinet job was startled and allegedly rather shaken at the volume of labour needed to do it properly. 'Ashen faced' was one elder man's description. Major himself when at the DHSS had explained to David Rodgers, his former neighbour in Beckenham, that a departmental minister needed to know when to say 'stop' to 'the paper and events crossing his desk at an alarming rate.' He had to be able to say, 'We know as much as we can and we must take the decision and send the information flowing back down into the civil service.' Those guidelines applied at the chief secretaryship with especial force. At the same time he was given to quoting Michael Fraser the former head of research at Central Office: 'A minister should always give the impression that there is all the time in the world, which there never is.'

Because the post also required good human relations, and because he was dedicated to good relations, he would enjoy good and sympathetic terms with all the argumentative spending ministers, with one spectacular exception. Between John Major and Nicholas Ridley there appears to have grown up a real and intractable two-way personal dislike. This, exceptional in Major, quite common with Ridley, would cause difficulties. In due course the Chancellor, exceptionally in a very smooth Star Chamber-free estimates round, would intervene to soothe the encounter. Though civil servants remark that the oddity of Ridley was his desire to *cut* spending, he is a man with some genius for disharmony. As a member of the present Cabinet put it, 'Ah well, that's not surprising, what with John being at the Treasury and him not being at the Treasury.'

In his time as Chief Secretary, Major understandably kept clear of other Treasury matters. He did not intervene with a view of taxation or interest rates or indeed the EMS. Terence Higgins, former Treasury Minister, who knows the custom and practice, makes it clear that this is the usual way with Chief Secretaries. They are too busy for macro-economics. Major was firmly loyal to his chief but very reasonably preoccupied with the mix of diplomacy, fast learning of other men's expertise and financial curtailment, which constitute the Chief Secretary's own specific job.

One civil service observer of the two men makes a contrast between them as it emerged at the budget meetings bringing Treasury ministers and advisers together. 'Nigel always had a very clear vision of what he wanted to do and was very gung-ho about doing it, though he says things as certainties now which one has seen develop. John Major, quite apart from having his plate very full, never wanted to talk as a theorist about general ideas. He wasn't interested in the broader issues, though he may have discussed them privately with the Chancellor.'

However, according to one well-placed witness, Judith Chaplin, his political adviser, a difference of philosophical outlook with Lawson perhaps existed over tax. Major gave the Chancellor support over his tax cuts and 'echoed the Conservative Party's rhetoric and reasoning about such reductions – the notion of money earners as the engine of the country and the fact that *more* revenue is raised on lower standard rates.' But, she says, he had a slight gut feeling that there were a lot of people doing visibly pretty well. One would then show him the figures again and he would accept but not be an enthusiast. Lawson of course would have had no problems, he knew that he was making the cuts and that was right.

The same observer remarked on 'never having known him do something he knew to be positively wrong just to please public opinion,' and had known him make stands on issues, though he had granted tax relief to workplace nurseries. 'Rationally,' she said, 'this was a gratuitous plus for the better off and it wouldn't have been granted but for outside pressure. It went completely against Lawson's philosophy of fewer taxes and fewer benefits. It amounted to a small lollipop. As a general rule Major wasn't willing to do something he thought mistaken, but he would pay popular error the wise compliment of very tender handling.

A quality discerned in him at this time by civil servants working with him was the belief that too cavalier a view is taken of poor people, that mandarins and ministers alike would see a sum of money as objectively small, when if lost to a poor person by some adjustment or denied by some frugality it would be quite large. He knew the people to whom a pound a week's change was actually important. He was also exceptionally responsive to the ungifted. 'Not a social Darwinian,' said one civil servant warmly.

He responded to the suggestion of disallowing social security payments to people not taking up training by saying, 'What about the youngsters who can't cope, who just don't have the mental capacity to sustain a training programme?' Officials fell about nervously and suggested referral to the DSS. 'But *they* haven't thought about it,' he said, 'so go back and ask them what they're going to do about it.'

'Socially,' said one civil servant, 'he is much nearer Chris Patten than Nicholas Ridley.' He would seem to include the ungifted and the losing side in his constituency. He was also noted being very sticky towards arrangements, like some from the Department of Trade which might make things easier for fat cat elements, observing that sums involved could better be spent on social security.

He was happiest of course sticking to the top man-management he was doing, and had always done, very well. It was accomplished by knowing all the facts and then meeting ministers and forcing them into compliance by being nice to them, but by doucely bringing up all those facts and details. There are recollections of his firm impressive deployment of evidence in discussion with George Younger at Defence, tackling the question of military extravagance. In fairnesss as to his success which impressed by dispensing with Star Chamber or arbitration procedure, he did enjoy an easier stretch of the cycle when Treasury demands were less onerous than at other times.

Part of his approach was to concede earlier some of the better points of the spending minister, not getting into unnecessary squabbles. Equally with a rather dramatic minister in a small department, Peter Walker for example, always fingering his resignation, he would surrender the small sums involved as not being worth fighting through the three-act performance. There is also a sly civil service observation that the quality of the minister didn't make so much difference to business, whether it was Leon Brittan, the most outstanding intellectually, Peter Rees who knew nothing and just used to say that he reserved his position, John Major the natural conciliator or John MacGregor who was quite belligerent in the job. Things roughly happened as they were going to, the point at issue presumably being the amount of political trouble stirred up in its despatch.

But what the Treasury preferred was someone who, putting the case, also understood it. And for all their self-sufficiency, Treasury civil servants showed their feelings when one of Chris Patten's people at ODA, in attendance for that sub-department's little deal with Major, looked at the assembled pictures of previous Chief Secretaries and asked, 'Who was the best?' 'This one,' was the unhesitating reply.

He was also winning real regard, affection is more the word, among his civil servants. He was seen as 'quite exceptionally nice, a friend, someone you would talk to in the corridor and love working for.' He would eat with civil service colleagues, going out for the occasional meal with them (pie and beans is mentioned by Nigel Wicks as his staple). He would maintain contact by letter and phone call with civil service friends, by no means all exalted, if they were away as one was on a Scholarship to Berkeley University in California.

He would also slip off to the Oval in the free moments of a busy life with fellow cricket enthusiasts among colleagues. Jill Rutter, the scholarship girl, recalls his organization of the mornings on Test match days to catch on TV the end of morning sessions. Jill, a member of Surrey in her own right, was obviously on the right wavelength. But her successor Carice Evans, a Welsh girl benighted on the subject, once brought the entire Chief Secretary's office to shocked hilarity by the question, 'Who is this Bradman?' He got to see less cricket as Chief Secretary than he did as Chancellor but then Chancellors have more time for serious thinking.

Quite seriously, since the Chief Secretary's job is to battle on the minutiae of someone else's programme, say housing benefit or hospital programme funding, he would spend much of his time in cabinet committee in a minority of one (two if the Prime Minister is there) and it would be contentious because it would not otherwise have reached cabinet committee. It is also a job with a rapid turnover of work which dictates the schedule. This is in contrast to the Chancellor who has a lighter schedule of meetings.

The life of a Chief Secretary, though full of work, was more carefree in one sense. There was very little security, he personally was little known and less recognized: 'the most anonymous role in government,' says Jill Rutter. She notices, like so many from Ken Livingstone onwards, Major's dislike of publicity, his avoidance of gratuitous appearances on TV.

She also observes the extent to which he actively enjoyed the House of Commons. 'Whenever he went across to vote he would say, "I'll be back in ten minutes." Twenty-five minutes later officials would be wondering where he was. He is incapable of going over and just voting. He'd be talking to people and enjoying it. Messages would be going out saying, "where are you?"'

One gory and pungent event that touched on the encounters between Chief Secretary and spending ministers would be the false move which ultimately brought down John Moore, DHSS secretary at the same period. A well-placed witness expresses uncertainty as to whether it was intentional. Moore was against universal child benefits; on the whole Major was in favour of them because of his serious concern about poverty, but he also knew what was politically possible. John Moore committed himself, says a critical witness, to 'flying along, blind, and wasn't stopped until he was brought right down. If he had been talked to earlier by people with other views he might have been saved from himself. He was allowed to run politically unsustainable things until they destroyed him,' adds the witness.

Treasury civil servants, among others, reject this. They note Moore's own Treasury background and willingness to pre-empt Treasury requirements. If a Secretary of State did that, a Chief Secretary could hardly tell him nay. The too zealous Moore was also unlucky not only with his own illness and the exceptional forensic skills of his opponent, Robin Cook, but from the season of outrage, the Birmingham heartbreak baby and other public misfortunes in which he had to make his stand. He was also too reliant upon the favour of an unsentimental Prime Minister and too early gilded in the eyes of his peers and party.

But Major would not be indefinitely engaged in the busy, largely happy activities of the Treasury. Mrs Thatcher with her unhandy housemaid's talent for treating friendship like best china, had just dropped Geoffrey Howe. An aching detestation of political Europe, not just the rational caution which might shy at some over-integrating impulses, but a profound unsympathy with non-American foreigners, and something close to hatred for 'the Belgian Empire' as she called it and the combative Catholic, Socialist and conviction politician Jacques Delors, had brought Mrs Thatcher spittingly to the boil. Geoffrey Howe, once close to her was now trading with the enemy, he was committed to the European thing, pushing for the ERM.

To a degree only historians with a long perspective will measure and explain how a loathing for Europe and the friends of Europe had grown in her. She wanted to be rid of Geoffrey Howe and after a day's pettifog, about alternative employment and suitable country houses, she *was* rid of him. She wanted at all costs not to hire in his place Douglas Hurd whose Europeanism made Howe look like a daytripper to Ostend. She would have neither ERM nor Douglas Hurd. To his amazement, she turned to Major, of whom it was observed that no one knew *what* he thought about Europe. He was in the Cabinet, he was sound on public spending, she liked him personally, he was not Douglas Hurd, he should be Foreign Secretary.

It is the measure of Mrs Thatcher's palsied touch at this stage that within a year she would endure both Douglas Hurd and, at the insistence of John Major, membership of the ERM! She was moving smartly down the long slide from fitness for office, but for mostly wrong reasons – she had made a good choice, the choice of her eventual successor.

9

Foreign Office

A colleague of mine, one of our outstanding journalists though not a Foreign Affairs specialist, passed on neutrally without making judgments himself, 'the views of all my establishment friends.' Those views apparently were that 'as Foreign Secretary Major was a disaster, had to mug it all up, was badly shaken by Thatcher's imperiousness when he was in Kuala Lumpur for the Commonwealth conference, was made to look like her poodle and behaved badly there.' He was unhappy at the Office they thought, and it was conceded by these establishment friends that he might have suffered because of the social pressures of the Foreign Office towards which a man might be forgiven a certain chippy resentment. Another source quotes the injurious statement that Major 'had to be taken to a map and shown where the world was.'

John Major himself expresses genuine astonishment and fervent dissent. One does have to make the judgment that a particular individual, resentful of the sudden promotion, a touch hysterical and talking far too much, appears to have babbled a good many highly subjective things which went via the dinner table into the establishment and gossip column pool of unevidenced certainty. As for the individual babbling, he retains a place but inspires the thought, 'So young, so fair they say, seldom live long.'

The Prime Minister points out that if he had been unhappy at the FCO he would not be bringing his diary secretary, Sandra Phillips, and his private secretary, Stephen Wall, from those days to Number

Ten to do respectively the equivalent job and to replace Sir Charles Powell.

His very first duty at the Foreign Office was to hurry off to Paris for a conference on Cambodia, he had the boat people to worry about (trouble from the UN commissioner on refugees) and of course the *ewige* EC. He did not care for the vast football pitch of a room given him which sounds like the one employed by Hinkel in Chaplin's *The Great Dictator*. He was not governing the Indian Empire, was his mild complaint, and he had himself moved to something on a more human scale.

Another aspect of the human dimension was a taste for shirt-sleeves. Many of the great mandarins who came to see him were apparently happy also to take their jackets off and do business over tea and biscuits. He was conscious that too much business flowed across the Foreign Secretary's desk. He was anxious that some of this should be delegated partly because junior ministers like William Waldegrave deserved more opportunity and because such centralization seemed 'ludicrous' to him.

He is not fazed by charges of 'having to mug things up'. Anyone in a new discipline would by definition have to absorb great amounts of untreated information. A few weeks after his appointment he went on what might technically be called a holiday, staying with Tristan Garel-Jones in his Spanish home. He speaks of taking 'huge piles of reading about the whole world and every aspect of Foreign Office policy' and immersing himself morning to night throughout the whole of August. He had position papers, treaties, details of ongoing negotiations, current dealings with the EC, the state of play on Hong Kong; he re-read himself into Latin America where he had been. He went into 'personalities, political complexities of politics, historic background and real underlying causes, possibilities of alliances, the information for competent reaction when events occurred.'

It wasn't, he said, 'a matter of finding out where the Isle of Wight was. That was clearly far beyond me.' He rejects the notion of poor relations with individual FCO civil servants, he took to some more than others but he is not the sort of man given to rubbing people up the wrong way. It is his style, given a difference, to reserve his position and decline to engage. There were no great flurries. What might have caused some frustration was his preference for sending for the specialist in a specific topic rather than his chief, the deputy secretary and head of a department. If he wanted to know about Equador he would ask it of the Equador desk officer, who would have those details rather than the deputy secretary for Latin America who would only have to ask the desk officer himself. He saw the senior man only when he wanted grander strategic information. Deputy secretaries ought to have something else to do and it was ludicrous the way everything made its way up to the top. (Actually this approach was warmly applauded by a responsible civil servant as the sensible way of doing business.)

He was not at all pleased, again contrary to the gossips' legend, to leave the Office. He was beginning to come to grips with it. He did not feel uncomfortable, he did not have great disagreements with officials. Perhaps, he thinks, some officials and many press men may have been disconcerted that he was young. There was something of an elder statesmanly tradition there; Bevin, Macmillan, Douglas Home, Stewart, Callaghan, with the first draft of Anthony Eden and the apparently unhappy David Owen as the only young Foreign Secretaries.

There are good reasons for thinking that the received version of the best publicized episode of his Foreign Secretaryship is grossly wrong. According to the legend which had better be set out: inexperienced Foreign Secretary is dragged at chariot wheels of great Queen to Commonwealth conference, is obliged to speak her words against South African sanctions, bullyragged by assembled post-colonial politicians he attempts to sweeten the British tone, accedes to some of their requests and is then humiliatingly made to recant by furious Thatcher, and then himself stalks off in temper, proof of inexpert placeman obliged to play poodle to mile-high Ma.

Better information is that Major and Thatcher consulted over lunch on the plane out and he made the suggestion that the South Africans were moving towards reform. The expression he used was 'I'm inclined to offer a bit of carrot as well as stick.' They agreed but did not have a line on detailed negotiations. When those negotiations followed with Commonwealth Foreign Ministers under the chairmanship of Canada's Joe Clark, they were rough and torrid. And

Major reckons he 'did not have a friend in that room,' at least on the South African issue.

He had hard-bitten exchanges with the Australian Gareth Evans, sledging perhaps? The relationship is described as being 'ropey' and involving 'very severe brushes' though they are friendly enough now. The negotiations went on for about seventeen hours and were of the line-by-line, minutely disputed sort. Major recalls four points at which he was not prepared to take a joint stand in a communiqué and expressly reserved the United Kingdom's position, using the formula 'Commonwealth ministers, with the exception of Britain, believe ...'

Mrs Thatcher was shown the draft and 'she did not change a word.' He and she discussed the communiqué and agreed that they ought to add a positive statement of what Britain did believe – anything else would have left dissent hanging rather sullenly in the air. At all times, Major as Foreign Secretary was a consulted party who agreed that the express British messsage should be put out. He is not sure whether he was the first to suggest over the lunch he had with Mrs Thatcher that it should be done, but believes it may have been him.

Unfortunately, he and Mrs Thatcher were in different buildings, both when drafting, over which they consulted over the phone, and at the time of the press release. He was next simply unable to persuade British correspondents present that there had not been a unilateral repudiation by Mrs Thatcher of what he had done. He insists that the press, having ignored his account of things to them, simply made a mighty collective assumption about another Thatcher ministerial row. (All this happened of course in the shadow of the real quarrel with Geoffrey Howe.)

Nothing that had occurred in Kuala Lumpur persuaded him or Mrs Thatcher that the matter even warranted discussion on the flight back. He arrived home to read 'great headlines to say we had a monster row and that I had stormed off in a fury. It was total rubbish, total rubbish from start to finish, it simply never happened. The press reports were 100 per cent wrong.' And he reminds us that it was days only after this event that Mrs Thatcher made him Chancellor.

There is no reason to disbelieve Major's account of events, in

Kuala Lumpur and at the Foreign Office generally. An intelligent non-specialist will indeed spend a lot of time reading himself intensely into the brief, he had not been a social security specialist when he joined the DHSS in 1985, or a public spending technician when he was appointed Chief Secretary. The conversational glissade which brings one from 'non-expert briefing himself' to 'amateur mugging it up' is only accomplished by malice. And of the existence of certain specific malice there can be little doubt.

A sensible civil servant, Richard Gozney, who saw a good deal of Major when working to the Minister's private secretary Stephen Wall (though he was not involved in Kuala Lumpur), expresses unselfconscious astonishment at the legend and says that he simply doesn't understand where all this comes from. He also gives a description of the new Minister's early days in the Office. Major asked for the pressing issues that concerned Hong Kong and China and made an immediate study. He showed every sign of rolling up his sleeves, having specialists down at once for the weekend to Huntingdon so that they could work on the issues together.

Generally, what he showed in response to any question was rigour. 'He did not rush to make up his mind and we would have worried if he had, but once he had resolved on a position he was decisive about it.'

Gozney also recalls a trip he took to Chartres for an informal gathering, 'without flunkies, just one bag carrier,' with EC Foreign Ministers. He prepared for that by prior contacts with at least two of them, Roland Dumas and Hans Genscher he thinks, as well as consulting John Kerr, then the FCO's Under-Secretary for EC Affairs. The only score against Major on this trip was that it confirms his Treasury image as a lover of plain English food. 'The French cuisine there,' says Gozney wistfully, 'was exquisite. But it was wasted on him.'

There is no support of any sort for the notion of the FCO not liking or respecting their Minister. Indeed the impression forms that popular, respected and well liked as Geoffrey Howe had been in his long tenure, Major's habit of standing back, taking in all the options and then reaching a firm conclusion, was appreciated as more decisive.

The office also took in the fact that over Europe he moved very steadily being far too pragmatic by nature ever to be either a sacramental European or a nagging resenter. He would, after all, as Chancellor set about the essentially diplomatic task of meeting virtually all the EC Finance Ministers and getting on all fours with them at personal level, all of which suggests a congenial FCO approach happily assimilated.

Most of the hostile talk follows from pack assumptions. Kuala Lumpur is a superstructure built on the first bad press, but it was of course intensified in the orchidaceous atmosphere following the Howe eviction, one sustained by the hot breath of the Lawson-Walters-Thatcher conflict so close to breaking. Against tittle-tattle one might usefully set a description of Major handling a head of state, Mr Vasiliou of Cyprus, who was under great internal and external pressure and occupying a vulnerable, harrassed position. Vasiliou waived his right as head of state to be visited at his embassy, came to the Foreign Office and was treated with such caring, well-briefed understanding by Major that having gone in depressed and wary, he emerged after three quarters of an hour greatly lightened in mood and giving Major complete confidence. This account fits perfectly the record of the sympathetic whip and the gentle-mannered Chief Secretary. The legend of a misfit out of depth and natural territory cuts jaggedly against the grain of probability. The two requirements at the FCO would be briefing, for which he has shown perfect aptitude throughout his career, and the handling of individuals, upon which his reputation chiefly rests.

Incidently if Major was unhappy at the FCO as he so fiercely denies, it seems odd that he should have made his London home on its top floor. During his time as Foreign Secretary he lived above the shop, taking one of the flatlets kept for duty officers. These are the bright young professionals who 'volunteer' for stretches of skeleton service, taking night calls which may involve helping the relative of someone killed or hurt abroad or may be an urgent call from a major diplomatic front. Geoffrey Howe was a little while debouching from Carlton Gardens, Major took the flatlet and, witness the dislike of being alone which his Treasury friends insist upon, hit it off extremely well with the duty clerks with whom he would eat cheerful non-exquisite breakfasts.

The one reservation he did have about the FCO was the loss of privacy. There is a great deal of security for the Foreign Secretary and Major dislikes not being free to walk about. 'It seems odd,' he says, 'to say that one got privacy at the Treasury but it's only money you run there not the world and really what is money?' He admits to being shaken by the hostile reports. Perhaps one might reasonably speculate that he will at some stage, without affronting Douglas Hurd, strike back by showing a greater involvement in Foreign affairs than anyone might expect.

Since Mrs Thatcher's alleged Kuala Lumpur conduct is the point of departure for a busy and distracting hare, this is perhaps a good moment for reviewing Major's relations with that lady. He had not quarrelled with Mrs Thatcher in Malaysia, though he would have unquestionable struggles with her about principles at the Treasury. She was a straight dealer saying what she thought and if she was on your side being so 100 per cent. He did sincerely like her and gives as one reason the fact that though she could and would and did mangle the great and the good, she never behaved badly or arrogantly towards unimportant people unable to answer back. (This is widely attested. Incidentally, as much is said about Rachmaninov who at rehearsals terrorized stars and nursed beginners gently along.) Major tells the story of a nervous young waitress at Chequers who, terrified, poured hot coagulating custard all over Geoffrey Howe's best suit at which Mrs Thatcher leapt up and comforted ... the waitress! One might aptly conclude that if John Major could happily handle Margaret Thatcher what credit can be given to the suggestion that he couldn't cope with the World?

10

Chancellor

As Chancellor, the post to which Lawson's bitter quarrel with Thatcher over ERM took him, Major, having moved through a lightening career zig-zag, would inherit a public expenditure white paper which he had written himself. He would also inherit the growing crisis.

He had been moved to that job as to the Foreign Office, because the Prime Minister, ever more distant from colleagues, thought of him firstly as Not-somebody else, first Not-Howe then Not-Lawson, secondly, as the Thatcherite, which except in terms of sincere personal esteem, he was not. She also hoped for an inexperienced, malleable Chancellor and someone who was far too young and short of accumulated office to be a threat to her. By means of such miscalculations, like Lord Randolph Churchill forgetting about Goschen, history happens. John Major was indeed inexperienced, but none of the other qualifications for comfortable subordination quite came to apply.

Comparisons would inevitably be made with Lawson who, reminding many of Denis Healey, had wanted to lead intellectual debate or unarmed combat. Major liked to use a Mills board with a line drawn down the sheet of paper to accommodate the pros and cons offered by civil servants, directly asking their opinions before he expressed any. One observer remembers Treasury people not in any way sneering at this even if they didn't put him in the intellectual league of Lawson, reflecting that he had the sort of Attlee qualities which the Treasury perhaps needed.

When he came into the job, he was plunged at once into two major speeches in the Commons: one on the economy, followed the same week by one on Europe. It was essential that he should do well to make his mark. Nigel Wicks, scrupulous in the rational Treasury mould, was closely involved with the European one. He puts the matter far less tepidly. 'He was a treat to work for. He would listen, he would say what he wanted, kick it around, and despite having already come in tired from the Foreign Office, gave two very workmanlike performances in the Commons.'

He wasn't seen by Wicks as a minister who ever let his guard down in debate; others might scintillate more but, in cricketing terms, they would leave the crease. Major always kept a back foot down. On Europe he was well aware of the explosive potential within the Conservative Party and without talking pap, he was keeping Europhobes and philes quiet.

In this light the view of his command as Chancellor given by Terence Higgins is highly relevent. As Chairman of the Treasury Committee, Higgins was able to compare him with predecessors and rivals and was impressed. The Committee is stocked with members who are quite useful, sometimes obstreperous questioners: the likes of Giles Radice, Nicholas Budgen and Brian Sedgemore. They have procedural latitude, three maybe four questions or supplementaries to a main question, put at some leisure with the usual Commons chamber tactic of smart terse irrelevance discouraged in the interrogated witness. The Chancellor would be accompanied by a couple of Treasury heavies, Peter Middleton and Terry Burns usually, but Higgins was taken by how little he relied on them, or, as was his right, passed questions to them.

'Imagine,' he says, 'the session they had on the hard ECU and European monetary union, a highly technical matter. It isn't easy to appear before a committee and in front of TV cameras for two and a half hours with virtually no reference to your senior officials.' He is very impressed by the ability to grasp and absorb detail. A comparison had to be made with Roy Hattersley who in his days as Shadow Chancellor would appear there. 'With all the effort he put into it, he was never really at home here.' Vastly more in command than Hattersley, Major made a better impression on Higgins even than the widely admired John Smith 'who tends to make funny speeches but doesn't have that kind of ingrained approach to it which normally does depend upon having a formal education in the subject.'

The received view in the Treasury was that given the frailty of the speculated-against pound, yet higher interest rates than the horrendous sixteen per cent we already had to carry were called for. The view at Number Ten was the exact opposite, in line with the Prime Minister's other obdurate conviction that there was no merit in entering the EMS.

The view of a close colleague was that in fact interest rates should have been put up six months earlier. By the time civil servants were bouncing the idea off the new Chancellor's head, it had become too late. Not everyone put his refusal to comply, his successful resistance to the manadrins down to the single brute fact of Mrs Thatcher's opposition. He was entrenched against her retribution. To lose two Chancellors would, after all, have looked like carelessness. So if he had been in agreement with his senior advisers he could have carried that policy against her. But he genuinely didn't agree with them.

His objection was characteristically half-political. By increasing interest rates the Tories became more electorally unpopular, something which of itself had damaged the pound (panickers and speculators selling against the day of a Tory defeat). We would, he thought, be back with a weak pound and yet higher interest rates. To make that stand, said the advisor, was courageous because before that the Treasury hadn't taken much interest in the way politics interacts on the pound. It wasn't thought the Chancellor's job. 'To come in and stand up against all his civil servants and say, "I don't want to do that," showed strength of character.'

Some hawkish officials wanted in the budget to bring about a sort of tax cut if only by not indexing personal allowances. The argument has been advanced that by not doing that he let the Retail Price Index go above nine per cent whence oil prices would carry it above eleven per cent. He had good political and social motives for not thus helping the better off but the half per cent increase on the RPI may have been mistaken psychology.

One departure as Chancellor was to put arguments previously

taken for granted, like the rejection of credit controls, properly through the hoops. Partly he was learning himself, wanting the same grasp of facts and arguments he had won at Social Security. He called in a series of technical specialists within the Treasury to reason such cases through with him. He set up small groups and asked for papers: 'a) to inform himself, b) to be sure that we had got the line right.'

He was not always responding with the Treasury's reflexes. Officials noticed a sympathy for manufacturing interests remote from the attitude once expressed by Jock Bruce-Gardyne towards 'the tie-clip making sector.' He was instinctively unhappy with a rentier economy, content with its holdings elsewhere. When he showed an interest in capital allowances for manufacturing concerns he noticed a senior official wrinkling his nose. The official explained why, 'What we permit in capital allowances is roughly what businessmen charge against their profits under accountancy rules.' And Major said, 'Ah that's a typical Treasury attitude.' 'He has,' says this official, 'a gut feeling that manufacturing, old-fashioned tin-bashing has a virtue in itself. You could give him a good case citing Switzerland where this wasn't the case, but he would feel it here (patting the solar plexus) that a serious country had to have a manufacturing base.'

Major, in a non-Treasury view, had been as Chief Secretary if anything very cool toward things European, if in a slightly flippant way, 'wishing that it would all go away.' He had become and was to become more strongly convinced about EMS, though his very early positive views, expressed in a parliamentary speech when he was a backbencher, had gone through revisions, recastings and changes of outlook in the interval. (One friend reckons he had actually forgotten about his backbench plea for EMS.)

Major was wholly awake to the deep split inside the Tory party, hence an earlier flip remark, 'I wish to God we were out of it.' Anyone who paid any attention to the Conservative Party at this junction knows that Europe was the one issue on which ardent partisans meeting you in the cloisters will pluck you by the sleeve, draw you behind a pillar and confide their fierce partisanship against the crazy Euro-fanatics or the pig-ignorant little Englanders. The split had (and has) replaced 'dry and wet' as party factions.

Major's own drift to Europe is hard to chart. He was surely influenced by Treasury minds who inclined to Europe; and very much like Labour Party politicians, he found the European politicans congenial, civil, moderate and a pleasure to meet. Mrs Thatcher's almost physical aversion to the conniving and sinister French, Germans and Italians was not widely shared across the spectrum. The 'Belgian Empire', which Nicholas Ridley had cacklingly reported to his office as something she said wouldn't last another ten years, 'was popular with many British MPs of all parties partly because of its amiable representatives and better natured politics.'

By contrast with so much prejudice, Major at the Exchequer set himself to know Europe by meeting those representatives. What the press gaily called a charm offensive was a mixture of finding out from EC finance ministers, explaining the British dilemma, not just the technical aspect of EMS but the expressly political hang-ups of his party. In Bill Keegan's phrase he was ending the practice of conducting policy towards the EC in the manner of a rabies control officer. And indeed in doing all this, he was also making friends. Further, in the view of his officials, he wanted to make up his mind. Europe they point out, is a difficult subject.

Travelling around and talking to foreign colleagues in their own offices was a way of doing it. With all Nigel Lawson's genius, such a course of asking, explaining but mostly listening, would have been unimaginable. The visits took in Pierre Beregevoy of France, Solchaga of Spain, the Portuguese Finance Minster, Wim Kok in The Netherlands, Henning Pedersen in Denmark, Christodoulou of Greece, Junker of Luxembourg, and he also met Guido Carli of the bank of Italy, elder statesman of European central banking.

The general view of his Europeanism taken by a range of civil servants was that he was friendly to it, subject to a distinct pragmatic gloss of being nowhere near a sacramental European. The words used to David Frost, that he was agnostic, have registered. He was not a convinced European idealist. But Major's position was that in no way could we leave the community. It was a source of conflict in his party but Europe was essentially a test of one's handling skill. And this implies involvement. The mechanism for goodwill in Bill Keegan's opinion was the Hard ECU, although Thatcher would later stick a knitting needle into it in the Commons with another of her ungovernable outbursts. It broadly served to shut her up on Europe, 'rather like a royal Commission,' he says.

Major's good relations with Treasury civil servants, an élite, but not a snob sort of élite, began to blossom. People like John Oddling-Smee, major begetter of the Hard ECU, Michael Scolar and Nigel Wicks worked happily with him. His taste for discussions, for learning and for not affecting knowledge of a given thing in a blasé, conning way, was winning a good deal of respect. As for the Prime Minister he agreed with her and had his struggles. He was showing her full loyalty, was genuinely fond and supportive but had moments of audibly clenching his teeth.

Accordingly then, he found himself siding with the Prime Minister against the mandarins over a further interest rate hike and with the mandarins against the Prime Minister over acceptance of the Exchange Rate Mechanism. In respect of the latter the supposition is that he very nearly gained a triumph in persuading her, as early as July 1990, to accept that we should join.

Finally of course in October his two balancing acts, Interest rates and the ERM, which we might call A and B, were turned to each other's account when Mrs Thatcher wanted a point knocked off A to impress voters and conference. Major was able to point out that the quid pro quo which economic gravity would require would be acceptance of B. However Bill Keegan believes that the deal was accomplished much earlier and quotes his own conversation with a Treasury official about when it would be safe to go on holiday without the big news breaking. 'When would he be going?' 'August.' 'That's fine, as long as you keep to August.' He believes that all the talk about getting inflation down before joining the ERM was spurious and that the Germans had said in the spring that going in was the only way to get inflation down, very much what has happened.

Anyway, with a gulp, both immediate objectives were accomplished and a single point fall in interest rates was offset by entry into ERM. The question which had stained the Government with the bad blood of Madrid and driven Lawson and Howe, furious and out of love, from office, had been resolved. Thatcher, according to one report, was more than reconciled at this point and was actually saying to Major and officials, 'Well, when shall we go in?'

Terence Higgins remembers a phone conversation with Chancellor Major on the night of entry into ERM and his own belief expressed then, that it was a proper rate at which to join, but a tough one in respect of downward pressure on inflation. You would then have to wait for the markets to *perceive* that inflation was coming down – not in the headline figure but the underlying level – before you could think of reducing interest rates. The only mechanism available to alleviate the pain would be some fiscal stimulation, not least the automatic stabilizers, when the increased spending on benefit goes through.

Major's previous autumn statement had implied that public expenditure would be inhibited – that is, not allowed to rise as a result of the recession. Subsequent statements to the Treasury suggested that this stand was being modified. The committee's draft report approved a 'clarification' of the Treasury position which certainly was not what it had been in the autumn statement.

The point made by Whitehall in respect of his refusal of an interest hike is that they noticed him qualify it very skilfully by pushing the time horizon out so that people did not expect rates to fall for a number of months. Psychologically, say the Treasury men, that is as effective as an increase, a tightening of policy without putting the rates up. They are also slightly awed by the sheer nerve of his sentence: 'If it isn't hurting it isn't working.' Not a phrase they admit that any civil servant would ever give a minister, it made its point and 'he got away with it. Perhaps,' they add wistfully, 'because it was true.'

Comparison between Major and his successor as Chancellor, Norman Lamont, may point to interesting contrasts in the future. Inflation and interest rates for example: both would be against inflation, Major because it would damage the party and hurt poorer people, but that his opposition would extend to getting inflation *lower*. Lamont would want to get it right down. And although Major had been tough on public expenditure, Lamont would be tougher.

Such social sympathy does not deflect the harsh criticism of hard bitten Keynesians. The account of Major and of the Treasury under the Conservatives of Bill Keegan must inevitably be more critical of both. The City Editor of the *Observer* has been a biting and elegant critic of the Howe-Lawson era and sees many chickens roosting in Major's time.

Keegan gives as his own view a sceptical notion of whether Major and his Treasury team can get things right. They had gone into ERM at the wrong parity (too high), and there was a balance of payments deficit which might be falling because of the recession but which was structurally there and wouldn't go away, even when our inflation and demand had outreached everyone else's. If you were joining a group within which you couldn't devalue, it mattered to get the exchange rate right. The starting point had to be realistic.

The division, he says, between the main body of critics and the Bank and Treasury was this: the critics said the Government, having screwed things up, had gone into the trenches at the wrong moment. Under Lawson they had let inflation rip in '87–'8 partly because they believed their own triumphalist propaganda. They were super-dedicated to fighting inflation in all circumstances and that if they gave up now interest rates would later go up may be to twenty per cent. And the people who believed this effectively had the Prime Minister screwed down.

There is, he believes, a mindset among Treasury people and their allies favouring a dark defile approach to the economy. A huge amount of unemployment simply had to be endured to get it right. He cites the humane neo-Keynesian Christopher Dow in his recent pamphlet as reflecting the wide ripples of this collective view. John Major had been reported as taking down the pros and cons of his advisers and was reflecting this outlook.

In very early 1991 the great body of advice Major would receive would be that high rates plus bankruptcies plus quantities of the jobless would work. The message from advisers to Major was, 'You can do it.' Keegan does not believe that he can. Such agonies endured at the wrong parity would not succeed. It was *his* certain view that the pound, even within the ERM, would eventually be devalued.

These are the subjective views of one critic and are presented as such, but they come from a distinguished source and if correct imply bleak economic terms for a long time. Alternatively, given Major's pragmatic impulse they meant an early election, which would give him the chance of devaluing after it. As things hang in the balance about election dates *and* the economy, all one can do is to respond to such comment and wait to see what happens.

For all his dissent from policy, Keegan has candid admiration for the style, charm, good nature and political command of the man. He describes a press conference at the last IMF conference in Washington in 1990. 'He did that gathering charmingly, brilliantly. I've never seen such a well-orchestrated performance. He had the foreign press eating out of his hand. And he comes across as not just extremely nice, but prepared to answer.' At the traditional Embassy party on the Monday he had, according to observers, worked the room, something startling to those familiar with the leisured and intellectually Caesarian ways of Nigel Lawson. 'In some ways,' says Keegan, 'it is odd to see a Conservative minister doing this. Because he is the ideal of what a lot of Labour people like – someone with no side, a man of the people wandering around without talking down or being ingratiating, just talking in a friendly way. Also he is quite funny.'

Keegan, having been critical in print about Major's cautious inaction at a time when he would simultaneously have been running very hard, was charmed with Major's comment at Tory conference in Bournemouth – 'This is the man who says I've been doing nothing all year.' Nothing can of course only be done properly with minute and laborious preparation. There was also Major's gentle remark on a Bournemouth hotel terrace where Bill had been sitting with a group of journalists, 'We're moving because we don't want to eavesdrop on a newspaper party.'

But the political aptitude accompanying this grace also showed up in an episode not appreciated on the City Pages of the *Observer*. His speech at Bournemouth had been 'pretty gruesome' – asking the audience to put up their hands to express disapproval of Labour. It had been awful, but this was conference and its effect on conference had been enormous. Hearing delegates say that this was their man, he felt that this bad speech had done all the work of Heseltine's four years of careful cultivation of the local associations.

The Treasury themselves, however vehemently they would differ from Keegan about the necessary wisdom of their deflation, see Major *personally* and *politically* in a remarkably similar light. The Treasury summing-up of his time at the Exchequer is that he used limited room for manoeuvre successfully, he improved Britain's position in Europe persuading the Europeans to listen to us and want to keep us on board, he got us through a difficult year when the temptation might have been to cut interest rates and run, he gave a somewhat softer image to the policy. Finally without anyone knowing – he may not have known it himself – he gave himself a political base from which he became Prime Minister.

Judith Chaplin, his advisor, recalls his conversations on the political future, all related to the scenario of Mrs Thatcher's voluntary departure at some uncertan time after an election. To that end he did his share of being available and socially on hand, in marginals as Central Office requested, but also in safe seats. But his relationship with Thatcher herself remained genuinely friendly. Hindsight, she points out, shouldn't obscure the fact that until very late and very suddenly there had been, despite widespread exasperation, no possibility in sight of Thatcher being toppled, as Michael Heseltine would topple her.

Treasury officials are fascinated by the politics. They don't think Major calculated the basebuilding beyond back-of-the-mind knowledge of longer term aspirations. They also see the built-in problems of any Chancellor also being a political minister. 'You can't,' they say, 'be a populist. You are regularly saying "no" and usually giving bad news. It doesn't make this a good spring-board to the highest job.'

They see his success in personal terms. 'He is not,' said one senior civil servant, 'an actor. Everything you see about John Major in the office or on television is John Major. Talk to him one to one, see him on the television, it's the same man. There is no acting there at all.'

It may be apt here to interpolate Major's own view of the Treasury. 'I love the Treasury. From the day that I first got into politics the job that I wanted was Chancellor. I will always regret that I wasn't Chancellor long enough to leave a mark on the job.' He was affronted by 'a snidy bit in the *Sunday Express*' alleging that he was not a great thinker or doer at the Treasury. He takes pride in having 'got us into the Exchange Rate Mechanism, presented the first televised budget, changed the whole culture of saving, changing the tax emphasis to savings rather than spending, the gift aid scheme talked about for forty years and not done,' also for the Tessa scheme.

An anecdote is told around the office. He was seeing a visiting foreign politician, not remotely one of the big ones. He was given a brief with all the details. The expectation of advisers was that ten minutes before he would have read quickly through the annexe with the essential bare figure to have a few talking points. 'No, he'd read through the whole damn thing and knew it. I suggested that it was a waste of time taking so much trouble in that much detail. Major said, "But if this man is coming to see me it's only courteous to know the detail." '

'He was', they say, 'given to getting up early to read such briefs and in that respect "you could not have a better man." At the same time, he would log this information without being made dull or tedious by it, see the wood in the trees and use it.' A recurring point of this narrative, whether it concerns Lambeth Housing Committee, Huntingdon Constituency, the Whips Office or the Department of Social Security, is underlined again.

Treasury people also found him able to make his mind up. They cite the European Bank of Reconstruction now to be sited in Britain, a difficult negotiation involving all the G7 countries. A lot of quick decisions were involved. He happened to be out of the country. 'You would ring him up on the other side of the Atlantic and put the facts to him. He would not spend time on going "Ooh ah." He could make up his mind all right.'

Treasury people are certain that he was happy in their department, enjoying its Periclean qualities. Nigel Wicks makes a point comparing it with a particular Cambridge college in which Nobel prize winners expect to have serious civil arguments with junior research fellows. An HOD principal could if able to make a decent case and be courteous, argue with him, the Second Secretary, under the nose of the Chancellor. Wicks alludes with admiration to the Mills board and its sheet of paper with the line down the middle. 'As we argued among ourselves, he would write comments, some on one side, some on the other.' He was listening to debate and making up his mind in his own way and time.

There is very little doubt as to the warmth felt towards him in the Treasury. 'We were very sorry to lose him but extremely glad he got the Prime Minister's job.'

11

Leadership Campaign

A view has been expressed, with nothing like evidence, that in some mysterious way Margaret Thatcher's fall was not what it looked like, the culmination of a period of spectacularly poor judgment by her, quarrels with foreigners, heel-diggings at the EC, and a breakdown of normal give and take with senior colleagues. There had also been such lesser but indicative things as the sudden lunge-and-screech attack on the new reformed Wilson-and-Water Labour leadership when she informed Mr Kinnock and the viewing nation that he was 'a crypto-communist'. The wonder with a leader so poised on the hair trigger of her emotions, is not that she went but that she took so long.

At the heart of Thatcher's defeat, the quite inadequate support amassed against Heseltine, the real triumph of his vote, lay her own recent actions, the acute unpopularity of the Tories. This had been highlighted by David Bellotti's electoral triumph at Eastbourne and, a point made over and over to me by different witnesses, the sloppy and inadequate campaign fought by her team. This involved the retired Defence Secretary, George Younger, and her PPSs Peter Morrison and Mark Lennox-Boyd. They failed, incredibly with an electorate of 371, to reach everyone and when they did served up the fatuous promise, 'She will change, you know,' to which as one MP put it, 'There were two answers, one, it's too late and two, no she won't.' The fact that sixty MPs had told the whips a year earlier during Anthony Meyer's candidacy that they would vote for her that time but could not be counted upon the next time round evidenced an element of probation in her support.

Mark Lennox-Boyd, a lugubrious man with a passion for talking shop like a slowed-down dental drill, would particularly enrage nervous and mobile voters by an air of impermeable and dismissive insouciance. The Thatcher people seemed charmed by their own projected figures which in the way of those about to lose were too high. Thatcher's own departure for Paris at the height of events did exactly nothing to help. As Jeffrey Archer, a sincere enough admirer, observed, 'She should have hired the toughest available whips and had them out twisting arms, knifing and threatening murder' while calling off Paris and throwing teas, dinners and at homes to charm the haverers, then she might have finished up fifteen votes above the safety line.

Ironically, of course, if she had followed this sensible course and scrambled into such a narrow lead, the position of the Conservative Party would have been vastly worse. A leader would have been registered as unpopular, then clung to power from a narrow ledge trying to assert continuity in the teeth of forty per cent dissent. Some of the wrangling and pettyfogging now coming from the posthumous Thatcher camp troubling us with tales about Heseltine voters misleading canvassers, misses the point that the effect of the vote was to save Thatcher from the humiliation of life as a political Struldbrugge outliving her political faculties.

We were saved a Thatcher 'victory' and witnessed instead a delicious chaos, the pre-order when a new state of affairs has to be fashioned. In such circumstances everybody is fixing, flitting, calculating. The business is to find a leader one doesn't actively dislike, who has a good chance of winning an election and, if the luxury can be afforded, may actually have some merit. Equally, this state of affairs, running from 6 p.m. Tuesday through to late Wednesday night was foreseeable as very likely. So of course that contingency would be talked about avidly by possible runners, their friends and the voters. Such contingency speculation is treason only to those with feudal notions of leadership.

Once the Heseltine score had registered on the Tuesday (20 November) ordinary business broke down. One unexcitable witness spoke of 'cabinet ministers abandoning their departments, followed by their senior civil servants.' Robert Hayward the MP for Kingswood, says that the Conservative party from Tuesday evening through Wednesday until the announcement of the climbdown, 'could fairly be called a bunch of demented ferrets.' The ordinary rules of courtesy broke down. Politicians were fleeing tables and companions in tea room and Harcourt room to rush across to possible bearers of fresh news, to other colleagues who must be pulled aside and consulted.

The pretence, central to politics, of not politicking had broken down. It was possible, he says, to see a gaggle of people including a particular one of cabinet ministers, openly caballing together. Michael Howard, the Employment Secretary, passing such a group, asked what they were up to. 'Oh,' said one lightly, 'we're just discussing the weather.' 'Whether she goes or stays,' said someone else.

Hayward himself is important to events. An amateur and dedicated psephologist, he had won much note during Sir Anthony Meyer's trial run in forecasting a total of sixty votes (for Meyer direct or abstaining). The final total, though somewhat differently made up, was sixty. He also speaks with some scorn of the Thatcher campaign group for the figure of 220–25 which they had offered all comers on Mrs Thatcher's vote at the first round. 'That was,' he says, 'totally unrealistic,' his own calculation, slightly understating the lady's final 203, was 200. Hayward's method was to go through the list and allocate people according to known views, friendships and prejudices. This is possible given that one is working on a small electorate of 371, most of which one has known individually for a number of years, an electorate moreover which is collectively in the trade of avowing opinions. As he points out one is judging people over seven years, knows whose PPS they have been, where they stand on Europe, or the Poll Tax, when and how often they have abstained or voted against. For example it was predictable that Edwina Currie would turn to Major. He had been her first whip, had run the bill on her first committee, had been turned to and given help, during her crisis at Health. Not being present to vote, she presented her proxy to Major with instructions to vote for himself.

A bright man like Hayward can if he wants be a small data-base in the House of Commons. And the last thing he would do, he indicates delicately, is to ask people direct. 'They would lie.' His facility with statistics was now well known and he was widely sought, especially after the first ballot result, notably by cabinet ministers, six or seven of whom wished to know his estimates. He does not say so but certain accelerated conversions to the cause of John Major by people not known by John Major to be his especial admirers, may owe something to Hayward's intelligence about the likely winning side. He did a calculation on the Tuesday night that in a second contest with Heseltine thirty to forty Thatcher supporters would defect from her camp giving Heseltine, on his arithmetic, a majority of twenty-two.

He was not of course the only one doing sums. By the time the second ballot was in prospect, the whips themselves had made a calculation. For they were facing that same question, now debated retrospectively and in *unbekenntnis*: the size of her support in a second bout against Heseltine. The whips had her losing or winning by a margin of five. But another calculation attributed to Michael Jopling, the former Chief Whip, had it that up to thirty members of the *Government* would vote against her on the second ballot. This, Hayward thinks too high but only because he had a substantial number of them voting against her on the first ballot!

His own calculations moved round the House with the velocity of a parcel in a Belfast pub and became general currency. Thatcher's second score against Heseltine was to be on the Wednesday, what the huddles of politicians, like the group of cabinet ministers crouching in the Aye lobby, were discussing, though perhaps not as feverishly as her own circle must have discussed it. Another figure which also preoccupied them was that of a division among cabinet members (at the Aye Lobby meeting?) also attended by the Chairman of the 1922. They allegedly split 12:7 against Thatcher standing a second time. This figure was quoted recurringly but John MacGregor, who was supposed to tell the Prime Minister, did not.

People were candidly preoccupied with successors, with Heseltine, Hurd and Major. The quite new PPS to Major, Graham Bright, told friends of receiving around 100 calls or contacts telling him to alert or inform his boss of support; and witnesses actually report other people coming up to Bright in the Lobby and openly bidding him to pass on to Major an urgent request under no circumstances to second Mrs Thatcher. The interest of ministers was intense and Chris Patten, catching Hayward behind the Speaker's Chair, asked him to take him through his figures. Patten's office was the site of 'an amazing parade of cabinet ministers and grandees' who had still to make the formal call on Mrs Thatcher. One of these was Francis Maude, soul mate of Mrs Thatcher who had decided that she couldn't win. It was said that Maude, facing the cruel job of telling her this, was 'ashen'.

All the numbers suggested a mighty prospect of defeat for Mrs Thatcher. Hayward going home on the Wednesday night after a Commons vote was convinced that she would go either that night or at the next day's 9 a.m. Cabinet Meeting. Actually people's responses to the voting demonstrated the much abused electoral system with its first-round requirement of a margin over plurality, as the sophisticated instrument it actually is. First time round, the Tories had really voted not simply for or against the incumbent, but on whether her position was practically tenable. Since it has been shown not to be, second ballot arithmetic about her performance simply gave the *coup de grâce*, the only coup in this election.

The next hypothesis was how would Heseltine perform against other people. Hayward, on both a trawl of the listed names and their loyalties and instincts, believed that Heseltine was beatable and had figures for it. The essential point was that although he commanded a substantial personal pro-Heseltine vote, the member for Henley had also collected a body of anti-Thatcher votes upon which he could not count. It also became the conviction of a number of MPs, notably the very influential Richard Ryder, that Heseltine would do less well in a field of three than against a single opponent. But Hayward argues at this time before John Major's surge, it was at least credible to argue that the beneficiary of a three-way contest would be Hurd. No ordinarily shrewd person, not even the astute Richard Ryder, could tell on the Wednesday night which out of Hurd or Major would prove the more popular in a contest, something which goes clean against any conspiracy except a Stop Heseltine conspiracy. There was no evidence says Hayward of the operation, perfectly proper at this stage, to hold quiet conversations checking support for a chosen candidate. Talking mostly among themselves Cabinet members were behaving a bit like Tattersall's ring.

No such common sense deflects conspiracy theorists anxious to believe that in some way they have been betrayed and that 'people she thought she could trust' were working against her. Norman Lamont, because of his dry economic views is seen as one conspirator; and the gossip columnist of the *Sunday Telegraph* attempted to rope in Peter Lilley, accusing him of having been present at the famous Catherine Street meeting.

Now that meeting was not itself conspiratorial and amounted to a group of people responding to an invitation of the Foreign Office Minister, Tristan Garel-Jones on the late evening of Poll Tuesday when Thatcher failed to win the outright majority, indicating a leader still even tenuously wanted by her followers. Garel-Jones had said, 'I'm going home now, anyone want to come for a drink?' Widely described as a dinner party it was said by one participant to be a dinner with the least food ever encountered. The subsequent talk-through at Catherine Street revealed two things, that among a particular group of younger politicians it was agreed that Mrs Thatcher was not placed to fight on and secondly, that despite some perfunctory discussion of other names (Tom King was mentioned, absurdly), they divided politely into preferers of John Major and Douglas Hurd and agreed tacitly that they must affably go their separate ways and work for those preferences. The gathering was made up of people on the centre and left of the party with a perfect moral right even before Thatcher was formally dead, of looking to her posterity.

In the case of Peter Lilley, a committed Thatcherite, attendance would not have been creditable, since he, a loyalist, would have been associating with a critical grouping during Margaret Thatcher's official political lifetime. For that reason he did not attend! Peter Lilley was in no way present at the famous St Catherine Street meeting. The *Sunday Telegraph* gossip columnist has made a mistake; whether or not he has apologised for this misrepresentation is not known. But armed with such standards of accuracy that column and its friends allege or imply prior planning by Norman Lamont. John Major is joined in the indictment on a nudge-nudge basis as, they suggest, obviously aware of what was going on.

In furtherance of this drift, a minor figure from the remotest regions of the far right, Harry Phibbs, an outrageous right-winger in his time with the disbanded Federation of Conservative Students but now working part time for the *Evening Standard* Londoner's Diary, rang round those working on Major's life, asking them a question. Was it true, asked Harry Phibbs, that both Norman Lamont and John Major, though giving out that they had voted for Mrs Thatcher and in Major's case seconding her, had actually voted against her? Such charges, as incapable of any refutation except the contemptuous denial they receive, as those of Senator McCarthy, come from a virulently conspiratorial view of all transactions and tell us most about the people making them.

But on the wider business of foreknowledge and conspiracy, it may clear the air of such furtive deep-breathing suggestions to offer the narratives of several people involved in those events. One account comes from an active Major group member, the Chairman of the Treasury Select Committee, Terence Higgins, a senior MP of dogmatic honesty and an unimpugnable witness. It carries rather more weight.

Events, he believes, were precipitated by Geoffrey Howe's speech, it was nonsense to say that that speech was the doing of his wife Elspeth (this is another piece of small-arms fire on the conspiracy circuit). Howe had had a very rough time from Margaret Thatcher, all third party evidence confirmed the fact. He finally decided that he had had enough. The speech precipitated the contest and the campaigns started. Higgins himself hadn't wanted an election and had indicated he would vote for Margaret Thatcher, which he did.

As far as Mrs Thatcher was concerned, 'the campaign was a very lacklustre affair.' There seemed to be no active attempt to canvass, at any rate so far as new members were concerned. The result of course came out while she was in Paris; it was apparent that it wasn't a very sensible thing, whatever the importance of the meeting, to have gone off to Paris in the middle of a leadership election. It showed a certain disregard for the importance of the issue and meant you weren't about to superintend your team or to call people in to meet you. However her announcement on the steps of the embassy that she meant to fight on was something to which she had no alternative. She couldn't have said, 'I'm going to think about it,' that would have handed it to Heseltine on a plate.

'Meanwhile,' says Higgins, 'John Major, having been informed that it would be a quiet week in politics, had retired to hospital for his operation.' The surgeon had described it as the worst case of a poisoned wisdom tooth he had ever seen. Indeed, Major had had problems with it right from the IMF meeting several weeks before and had been taking antibiotics ever since and thus their impact had not been very great. 'So while all this was going on he was still in bed.'

After the first poll the next step was the Prime Minister's consultation with colleagues in her room at the Commons. Higgins has a room immediately above the Chancellor's which is next to the Prime Minister's and, as he says, 'I go up and downstairs a good deal.' So 'there were members of the Cabinet milling around and looking into the middle distance. She had them in one at a time. Her question it became clear from conversation on the stairs was, "Are you going to support me?" And the answer, "Yes I am." Somebody raised the point that the right question to ask should have been, "Am I going to win?" That question was put and received a steady volume of negatives, and it was pretty well established from other sources that Kenneth Clarke indicated that he was ready to resign if she pressed on.'

That evening Higgins, forewarned about the Cabinet's confession of its pessimism to Mrs Thatcher, insisted to Graham Bright, Major's new PPS, that the convalescent Chancellor must be there the next day. (Higgins makes the point here that he was worried about harrassing someone more ill than had been thought, because when a Treasury minister, he had told a sick Iain Macleod *not* to leave hospital; he did and died.) He and Bright agreed to meet in Major's room early the next day, they were joined by Francis Maude, a Thatcherian junior Treasury minister and Richard Ryder, also at the Treasury. There was still no Major and at this stage no Norman Lamont (then Chief Secretary). Lamont finally turned up and took them all to *his* room. The television they kept on and suddenly it told them the news they had been gearing for – Mrs Thatcher would not be running. And just as that statement came over the screen John Major and his wife arrived from Huntingdon.

'It now mattered,' says Higgins, 'that, Cambridge Union style, the candidate was proposed and seconded, the papers filled in and delivered to the returning officer.' Lamont was to do the proposing but a minor problem occurred over the seconding – it was to have been done by Higgins, but as Major was due to give evidence to Higgins's Treasury Committee the next week, it might have looked odd (and doubtless exciting to conspiracy-hunters). So John Gummer, also now present, was put on to the form.

It was agreed to contact Douglas Hurd's people at this point, agreeing to make a joint statement saying that they were all good friends and would have a good clean fight which, says Higgins, it was. 'All this time Norma was pouring antibiotics into John.' The papers were put together and handed over to Graham Bright who got them into the hands of Cranley Onslow not so far ahead of 12.00 as to make for leisured comfort.

'At this point,' says Higgins, 'things took off.' The Major campaign at once acquired the use of a house in Gayfere street which runs parallel with Lord North Street on that pleasant cruciform pattern of streets running off Smith Square. It is, as Lady Bracknell would have put it, a very satisfactory address. A short saunter from Parliament, it is an even shorter one from Conservative Central Office; and for those with wider tastes, St John's Concert Hall and the Transport and General Workers Union are equally accessible. The headquarters were laid on by Alan Duncan, Conservative candidate for Rutland, a near neighbour of Major's. The Conservatives, not being a party of workers and peasants, are well placed to furnish such useful accessories. From here, with the leadership commuting to Number Eleven, office of the Chancellor, the campaign would be fought.

That house has however been another splinter of bone to the worrying dogs. Who but long prepared conspirators with their slow-matches lit and their bearded faces hidden behind cloaks could have been so well provided with just the nearby headquarters they needed? This can be no coincidence. Guy Fawkes, remember, worked out of a house convenient for the parliamentary cellars belonging to another furtive associate up to no good.

The reality is that all roads lead to William Hague. The member for Richmond, Yorkshire and Lamont's PPS is a close friend of Alan Duncan and actually stays at the house himself. His message to Duncan appears to have been on the lines of, 'Oh, do you mind if I have some chaps in to help get John Major elected?' Duncan came back to find thirty or more people bivouacked around his quarters. He seems not to have minded. Indeed the ready availability of office equipment, telephone lines and faxes was the result of the house being used partly for business by Duncan who was able to augment facilities from the same suppliers. Rob Hayward remembers breaking in to stop a colleague from waving away the chance of a fax with a shout of, 'No, no we're going to need one of those.' Everything was being made up as they went along.

The team running things had a core, Lamont was in charge, Maude and Robert Hayward were doing numbers with extra help from David Davis; Richard Ryder and Michael Jack were directing contacts and press connections, especially the individuals calling colleagues with a canvass. Higgins had responsibility for what were lightly called 'the urban squires', elder, wiser and senior members. The whole operation was exceptional for its good humour. Rob Hayward, ensconced in a basement room he had bagged at sight, complains only of the stench of humanity in tight propinquity but says there was, extraordinarily, 'not even a hint of short temper, not one wrong word,' no flaring up of anger or resentment despite a heavy schedule and conditions which could have brought in the factory inspectors.

One thing which helped him and the whole group was the fact that he and Michael Jack, deputies for numbers and contacts respectively, as close, long-standing friends, could substitute for their bosses in liaising about what one group needed next of the other. He was, by the way, particularly taken by the grasp and command of Norman Lamont, whom he had not previously known well. A problem of a good sort was the crush of people wanting to get involved. At one point there were fifty MPs engaged in ringing up 321 other MPs. Once one had deleted the people working in other camps and other ferro-concrete certainties, the ratio of canvassers to voters came down even lower than one to six, and people were, very nicely, being turned away.

On the Friday morning it was decided to call a press conference. (Higgins owns with a shudder to never having seen the entire trade of newspaper photography assembled before!) The most important question was one about Mrs Thatcher's threatened referendum on Europe. Major misheard it at first but managed eventually his first change of policy – effectively to bury this very ill-advised idea left over from the obsessive ultimate phase of the last regime. The much derided remark about a classless society (far more credible in the long perspective of Major's life) was also made on this occasion.

With five days to work, the team decided to arrange for their cabinet catches (senior ministers wanting to come out publicly for their boy), to do so one at a time on a daily basis. The only time this failed of impact in the media was the day when Howe and Lawson, making their joint declaration for Heseltine, took over Sunday. 'At the time we were more upset about this than we should have been.'

By pure chance on the Friday night Higgins was attending (with Tony Newton as his guest) his own annual constituency dinner in Worthing. (Newton's declaration for Major was being kept back until next morning.) Higgins had kept his constituents informed that if Thatcher should stumble at the first ballot, he leaned to Major. His confirmation of support for him at the dinner was met 'with acclamation'.

On the Saturday it all became hard work. Higgins remarked to his wife Rosalyn, that he had been in the Commons for twenty-five years but had now found himself in politics. It was becoming 'a straight Cambridge Union election with a slightly surreal atmosphere.' They were established in that bunker at 18 Gayfere St. They were also getting the invaluable help of 'a nice girl called Angie,' actually Angela Bray. On loan from CCO press office, she is everywhere described as completely knowing the score where newspapers, reporters and phone numbers was concerned and making herself more than helpful.

It was decided to organize a photo opportunity *outside* no. 18, wisely not letting the photographers in. As a result they appeared in colour on Page Three of the *Sun*, an honour which, like Juliet, 'they dreamt not of'. The photographs were good, though 'in better focus on the *Times* than the *Telegraph*'. The press had been put into very good humour by Major's setting out to talk football and the fortunes of various London clubs with them. Not since Tony Crosland went upstairs at parties to watch Match of the Day has there been such enthusiasm for the people's game in high places. (There is something of a sporting mafia in the Major camp – Lamont being a cricket buff, Mellor a Chelsea supporter and their advisor, Terry Burns from Co. Durham, another football fan. Peter Lilley observed that he wasn't really very keen on sport but that he affected an interest in cricket in order to remain socially acceptable at the Treasury.)

The group took especial care with their canvass. It was 'implacable in its standards'. No answer short of 'Yes I will vote for you' was counted in. People in the group undertook to ring those MPs they knew best. But the numbers being crunched by Francis Maude and Rob Hayward were telling their own story. Each man followed a different pattern, Maude was working out of the inflowing statistics, by way of a mathematical formula, deleting fifteen per cent off committed voters, twenty-five per cent off probables and fifty per cent off possibles; Hayward, out of the book on a seven-year knowledge of opinions and private loyalties. Interestingly, they were never, in a series of re-assessments, to be more than eight votes apart.

Multiple canvassing, says Hayward, was a worry because it was both irritating to subjects and liable to confuse the number takers. They were to shift on one run-through of members to a country basis: 'Jones do Middlesex, Robinson do Buckinghamshire.' This led to the ringing up of other people, like an irked Peter Rost, who thought *they* were working for John Major. To avoid such confusion eventually a central volume in a binder was devised by William Hague and looked after by Andrew Mitchell. Each MP had his own sheet giving the record of the canvass call to him, his response and whether further steps, like a call from a minister or indeed Major himself, were necessary. In this way truly marginal electors could be identified and targeted for the personal treatment.

The binder was suggested early Friday and was ready and available on Saturday morning. Hague and James Arbuthnot liaised with Major at Number Eleven, letting him know from Maude and Hayward with whom he needed to speak personally. No later than seven that evening Major had started contacting marginal and uncertain voters. But there was extreme difficulty at first getting through. But by Sunday morning, says Hayward, it was going very smoothly,

Hague and Arbuthnot having done very well.

Higgins reports that virulently *Thatchertreu* people who said, 'You have brought down Margaret,' were told, 'Would you like to chat with Margaret?' The outgoing Prime Minister, determined to stop Heseltine, had made her support for Major clear. At the same time, other people were being assured that Major was not the prisoner of the right. Norman Tebbit, who was able and willing to do a great deal for the Major camp, asked that his name should be kept quiet because he realized that with many people it would be counter-productive since he is the committed partisan of a faction. Other right-wingers who worked on their friends for Major were George Gardiner, Angela Rumbold and Eric Forth. Tony Newton and Robert Hughes were doing similar things in conversation with the party left.

This could be done with a perfectly clear conscience given Major's heterodox mix of views, but in a fight like that who is counting? A point to make in such phone conversations was the underlining of those polls showing Major able to beat Labour. The chats also had to see off a notion put by some leaderwriters, that Major was only putting down a marker in the hope of being next leader but one. (To any attentive watcher of Commons politics, that sort of thing merely illustrates the tragic genius of leaderwriters for narrowly missing the self-evident.)

Some people, sighs Higgins, ended up being called by two members, three cabinet ministers and John Major. The ringing went on and on until after midnight on the Sunday, catching people who had been out all day. Inadvertently someone rang the Heseltine Head Quarters and got an answering machine, something which gave a lot of quiet pleasure at the Major team's superior application.

By Monday the group was placed to say, perfectly truthfully, that they were within sighting distance of winning. The hard, promised Major vote was by then way past 150. It was also clear that Hurd, always vulnerable despite his wide field of respect, as being too *largo maestoso* for the break-dance of modern politics, was failing. Rob Hayward points out that the intakes to parliament of Tory MPs in '83 and '87, though by no means the batches of Thatcherite clones predicted, were notable for their low toff ratios. 'More Harrow teachers than Harrovians,' he says, meaning Robert Key and Andrew

Hunter. The Hurd camp, to its regret, had become excessively a resort of the patrician element. The Hurd element was also being squeezed by the preferences of constituencies visited over the weekend. These were very heavily for Major. His own with seventy-five per cent had been at the light end of such enthusiasm.

Because Hurd was evidently out of the race the focus of attention switched to the third ballot and its pre-emption. 'I put in,' says Higgins, 'an incredible amount of work on the Monday and Tuesday trying to see that people in the Hurd Camp were ready to vote for us and not for Heseltine.' Gayfere Street had made its own assessment of the split and allocated almost all the Hurd supporters to the attentions of cabinet ministers or near equivalents like Higgins or Archie Hamilton as best able to handle such a concentration there of seniority, office and importance.

A minor point at this stage concerns the publication by newspapers of lists of supporters. Since the reaction, 'If *he* is on your side, I can't vote for you,' is not unknown, this kept the assurance givers even busier. Though the fact that none of the three candidates was a supporter of capital punishment removed an extraneous motive for supporting one candidate over another. The campaign also took care to allocate its active members to various radio and TV stations to say how well things were going. David Mellor, one learns elsewhere, was the most heavily booked.

This campaigning continued through the actual voting on Tuesday. On that night, Higgins says, 'We were waiting with a very small group at Number Eleven, some of whom were walking round in circles, some of whom were walking up and down.' He takes pleasure in falling short by two, affording a chance for the opposition to concede with grace which, very handsomely, they did.

Asked directly about the conspiracy theory – that in some deep-dyed way, Major and Lamont knew more than they admitted and contributed to Thatcher's fall – Higgins replies that he thinks there is no truth in it whatsoever. There had been a serious danger after the first ballot that Thatcher might have insisted on going down fighting, in which case the party risked getting a leader it didn't want. A straight Thatcher–Heseltine re-match would effectively have ruled out other candidacies. Telling her that she wouldn't win was first true, and second it made a broader choice possible.

As for the speed with which the Major camp went to work, something of which the conspiracy people had made a great deal, 'It was pure spontaneous upsurge of enthusiasm, I've never felt anything like it. It just took off. The whole thing was just unreal. We were waiting up to get the early editions of the next morning's papers and then being back at work at 7.30.'

Anyone, Higgins argues, who did have conspiratorial thoughts wouldn't have anticipated that she would do that badly on the first ballot anyway. Heseltine took his decision to stand against her but that was hardly conspiracy. 'The only relevant accusations would be against Norman and John and I have no reason to give them any credence.'

At the heart of John Major's campaign, indeed its director, was Norman Lamont, a Treasury colleague and one close to Mrs Thatcher's views on the economy and especially on Europe. His account is central. He had viewed a defeat for Mrs Thatcher as a possibility, but his own first reaction to the Tuesday 20th vote had been that Thatcher, whom he had supported and voted for, could still win. But he had always feared that the electoral system which he thinks 'absurd' could make great difficulties for her. His wife Rosemary reminds him that he had said, 'If she doesn't get this first time she's in real trouble.'

Having made an immediate first reaction to the first ballot that she might win through, he soon changed his mind. He did so, he explains, as a result of taking reports from his PPS William Hague, other Treasury PPSs, other Treasury ministers and Rob Hayward, universally sought after for his political numeracy. That psephologist had the names of forty people who, having voted for Mrs Thatcher, now felt that the party was irrevocably split and that they could not go on. A second list (Michael Jopling's) a former Chief Whip, said similar things.

Lamont was also meeting ministers expressing this view. Anyway how would they explain in a General Election the fact that such a large minority didn't want her as leader? Continuation was simply becoming unviable. Given the view that he had now formed, he had talked during Wednesday with two or three Cabinet colleagues, Parkinson (early) Gummer and Howard (late at night) among them, and had been told that they favoured Major. This also proved true of Peter Lilley.

Lamont had attended the Catherine Street meeting. Tristan Garel-Jones had asked him for a drink, large numbers had also turned up. His mind was already made up by now. Everybody there was in favour of Hurd, he was the only supporter of Major and he put the Major case. He respected the Chancellor's competence and skill, while his views, interestingly, were those most compatible with his own. (One might do well there to note that Major is the least European of the three candidates.) Lamont liked Major, thought him decent and had been glad of his backing as a senior colleague. He also remarks a hard-to-identify quality by which a shunner of heavy publicity could make people like him in great numbers.

It had originally been intended that Norman Fowler should run the campaign but he withdrew. Lamont was initially just chairing the meeting and when John Major arrived *his* instinct was to dispense with any campaign chief, but little arguments about what to do and where to go and what should be the make-up of the proposers made it clear that somebody should make decisions, so *de facto* he took it on. Knowing that they wanted a press chief, he asked for Richard Ryder, Treasury, ex-whip, general good thing. He also wanted Angie Bray from central office, Francis Maude as Thatcherite and ex-whip and Hayward whose figure play had acquired utility chic.

They began the day with an eight o'clock meeting at Number Eleven to go over: the canvass returns, what should be said to the press, the figures and who should call whom. They were indeed, Higgins says, 'all having the time of their life and would be sorry when it was over.' So strong did their support grow, even with tight quality control on accepting promises, that even before the second ballot they were working on the disposition of the Hurd vote. There was to be, he says, 'a faint sense of let down after the result: they wouldn't be able to go forward with their plan for the third ballot because they had won!' They would of course before the end be doing too much, often several times. Virginia Bottomley grumbled that for the third ballot she had been canvassed three times.

On the day of the vote, expecting his man to be, by a degree, ahead, Richard Ryder had prepared separate speech notes for three conditions – narrowly behind, narrowly ahead and outright victory – in fact they would use the second, but the only one Major would concentrate on was outright victory. He was, says Lamont, very confident and half an hour before the count he was fast asleep in bed, a notable contrast with his expectant father, 'I'll lose, I'll lose' approach at Huntingdon in 1979. Lamont actually said, 'You think we're going to win outright?' and Major had said, 'I do rather.' On his own list Major inclined to greater optimism, counting as 'certain' names which others had marked 'probable'. He was right of course. Hayward admits to a final estimate twenty short, having prudentially cut his raw figures down.

Major's own instinct was to use television as his main weapon, rather to Lamont's anxiety. And he had to be affably bullied to do all the ringing round of haverers which his managers wanted of him. He took to referring to Lamont as 'That tyrant'. Tyranny took the occasional form of dialling the numbers for him and sticking the phone in his hand.

As for Mrs Thatcher's direct involvement as a willing reference for the new boy's merits, Lamont reminds us that that was made particularly necessary by the reaction of some of her supporters that they would vote for Heseltine! The further fringe of Mrs Thatcher's support contains a fair measure of paranoia to the square inch; the first roots of the will to believe in conspiracy start here. To rational Thatcherites the candidate was able to offer his actual need of them. Major was able to talk to George Gardiner of the right-wing '92 group along lines of, 'I will be more dependent on you than any other candidate.' In other words he would be more indebted.

If Norman Lamont is a vital voice one is even more at the centre of things. How does the new Prime Minister recall events?

The Prime Minister himself dismissing conspiracy talk as 'rubbish', explains the full extent of his illness at the time of the crisis. He had been due to go into hospital back in the constituency to have his wisdom teeth out. This had been planned for some time, something I can vouch for since he had told me of his exact plans when we had met for a talk in July 1990.

The surgeon was to tell him that he would need at least a week away and more rest since it was one of the nastiest cases of its kind he had seen. The tooth on one side was growing into the roots of the next one and he had suffered pain for some months. For such surgery he was, in the brutal terms of the trade, an 'extremely elderly patient'. Such considerations are apt to be preoccupying and he was in no position to contemplate plans or conspiracies. One of his reasons for not cancelling the appointment, apart from pain and an acute desire to be put right, was that the conclusion might be drawn that Mrs Thatcher was in crisis. He talked the operation over with his wife who was keen that he should have it done.

The day after the Tuesday ballot he spoke to Mrs Thatcher on the phone, agreed that he would be happy to continue to countersign her papers and they were sent to him. He was at this time feeling distinctly ropey, in and out of bed trying to read Jeffrey Archer's MS of his novel which the writer had presented to him. A cabinet minister (not identified) rang to say that he would be seeing Mrs Thatcher and that he would tell her she should not continue. Major was 'very downbeat about it' and said that he didn't think that was a good idea and advised against doing it. But he went ahead. 'Peter Morrison late that evening rang to say that he *thought* Mrs Thatcher would in fact stand down,' and would let him know more next morning. Morrison advised against his trying to attend the next day's cabinet meeting. He was rung before eight the next morning to say that definitely she would not be standing.

A number of people then rang wanting him to stand. He made it clear, he didn't know whether he wanted to stand, he had neither nominator nor seconder, he had no campaign manager and no campaign team. He set out and arrived in London about eleven o'clock and was waited upon by Norman Lamont and his group. Until then Major had not known that John Gummer or Michael Howard would be on his side in any potential conflict but they turned up. This small group made it clear they had a larger group of people who had contacted them. His papers were rushed over rather, as Major observes, like his hectic last-minute nomination at St Pancras North. They were brought by Graham Bright, his old friend and new PPS (Tony Favell a fervent Euro-doubter having resigned a few weeks earlier). Apparently they came as a perfect surprise to Cranley Onslow, Chairman of the 1922 committee and returning officer – 'he turned as white as a sheet.' One can't think why but then many things come as a surprise to Mr Onslow.

The campaign got off to one slip, Francis Maude called it but everyone went to a wrong venue. Even so, from a standing start after ringing, talking and adding up names on the evening of that Thursday of final nominations, a meeting of the group was able to contemplate a figure of 115 firm promises. John Major says he was dubious about such a figure but 'that is what they said they had'. 'There was no predetermination,' and that is the truth of it. On the previous day, the Wednesday, while he had been lying groggily in bed in Huntingdon, a number of people had telephoned his PPS to ask if he might stand. Graham Bright could give them no answer or comment, quite simply because he and Major had not discussed the matter. He had talked the matter over at home once it loomed. He was unsure; 'the children were unsure, to put it mildly.' He 'was not excited about it.' He could see that it might be unavoidable. However, in his own words: 'The excitement of the job and the capacity to do things ... yes, but I was very conscious of the loss of privacy ... It had hit us very hard the loss of privacy as Foreign Secretary, very hard indeed, all that security. The one thing I really loved when I left the FO and went back to the Treasury was that I got back a lot of my privacy.' His wife, Norma, had loved the period when he was at the Treasury. The Prime Minister concluded this discussion with the observation that he could understand Greta Garbo!

By way of coda to the accounts of the central player, his campaign chief and two other MPs, it is instructive to hear another witness, outside the Commons but able to report on Thatcher's last hours of power: Jeffrey Archer the successful novelist and former Conservative MP (Louth 1970–74) who works relentlessy for the Conservatives and has maintained solid links with both Thatcher and Major. Temperamentally the dramatic Archer must be as far from the cool Higgins as could be.

He had been asked by Norma Major to spend some time with John on his first day out of hospital when he would be groggy but would enjoy company. This was to be on the Monday after weekend hospitalization. Accordingly, Archer spent that day, the one before the first poll, nine hours in all, with Major. Major had talked to him at the Treasury during a brief call the previous Friday, before the operation and had said that Norman Lamont had advised him to postpone his operation because of the possibility of a Thatcher defeat. Norma Major had said she was very much against his staying out, she didn't want him to be thought so avid of office and she wanted him attended to.

At this point one should consider whether advising Major to hold back from hospital against the event of a defeat for Thatcher constitutes, even by the standard of zealots, any sort of treason. She might lose, in fact she did lose. The politician who foresaw that possibility and advised his departmental chief to be aware of it was seeing well and acting prudentially. Any sailor observing a hole in the ship has a right to look sharply to the boats. Lamont is an economic dry and shares Mrs Thatcher's unease about European developments. From that personal outlook Major would be the natural next choice if Thatcher should fail. To advise readiness for that possibility is not betrayal, it is a taking note of gravity.

Norma, when rung on the Saturday after the operation, had confirmed that she wanted him to come round on the Monday. He spent a good deal of time getting the papers from newsagents in Huntingdon. They read together a piece in the *Times* saying friends of Major wanted him to be available. Major simply said something about a week in politics being a long time.

Archer rang Major on the Tuesday after the result and was simply told that Major would be supporting Thatcher and went off to his Albert Embankment home. He was called next day by John Whittingdale, Mrs Thatcher's political secretary who was moaning about having nomination papers for Mrs Thatcher but no signature from the remote and convalescent Major, the official second as he had been from the start. 'Fine,' said Archer, he would get his chauffeur to take it up. Archer had to speak that night in Norwood of all places, a South London district where Major had once been an unsuccessful member of a candidates' shortlist. The chauffeur, Bob Slavin, was despatched to Huntingdon to collect the signature on the papers. Bob was expected back at 11 p.m.

At the expected time there was no Bob. Archer called, first the car phone, then the Major household. John Major in his usual courteous way hoped Archer wasn't angry, Bob was still there, 'not to worry but can't talk on the phone, understood?' Major eventually rang again to say that Bob was on his way, he couldn't say much but would talk to him the following day. Bob arrived with an envelope containing the paper at about 12.30 midnight. Archer called Downing Street and learned from Elsie on the switchboard that Whittingdale, Gummer, Morrison and Mrs Thatcher were in the building but didn't know where. He reached Whittingdale on the phone and said he wanted to get the papers off his hands into theirs.

Archer then puts things with a nice self-satirical touch of Mr Jingle. He personally had been away from the hub of events since 5.30 (and few places are further from any known hub than Norwood). 'You all know now what had happened. I knew nothing at all. Here was this man who only knew that he had saved the leader of his party, had done his bit for his country, a Dukedom was certain. I walk in, and there are Whittingdale and Morrison. Mrs Thatcher and Gummer are in another room preparing the speech for the no confidence debate. I handed the envelope to Peter Morrison and he took it and tossed it to one side, and carried on with the conversation. The significance is the tossing aside. If she had been standing – rip it open, check the names, get it into a file, see the chairman of the '22 gets it. "Do we want to ring Cranley Onslow now?" They did none of those things. The decision that she should bring it to an end had been made.'

Archer makes a claim for himself which should not be thought fanciful. He has been eating chicken for England for some years now on the Tory supper-and-speech circuit, addressing a minimum of 100 meetings a year. He is also a committed supporter of his neighbour, Major, and has been since the mid-eighties. Archer also reckons to have answered the recurring question, 'Who's next?' with a summary of pros and cons which always ended with, 'Long-term insider judgment is for this chap Major,' or some variant of that sentiment.

Jeffrey is a very popular figure in the constituencies and would be listened to. It doesn't seem extravagant to believe, as he does, that the heavy majority shown for Major among constituency chairmen, when they were asked by Lord Lane to assess association opinion, was influenced by his sustained and recurring insistence. Given the jumpy mood of backbenchers and the retributive mood of some local associations towards those who had defiled the covenant by voting down Thatcher, their preferences in turn would carry consultable weight at Westminster when Lane passed his figures to a meeting of the 1922 committee. Heseltine had not ridden bareback round the same circuit for no reason. Archer's advocacy was a specific but far from discountable factor.

His own immediate job during the Gayfere Street group's campaign had been to liaise with newspaper editors with whom he was well connected. On the Saturday he particularly wanted to learn who were they going to come out for. He was able to tell Richard Ryder the directions to be taken by a string of newspaper editors. One of them, David English, had said that the *Daily Mail* inclined to Heseltine – he wanted Major but his staff thought otherwise – 'Lot of Heselteenies in my office, I'm being bullied by them.' A likely story!

Archer would also convey the major piece of bad news to the group. A call from Andrew Neil passed the rumour, later confirmed, gathered by the old star Michael Jones, that Howe and Lawson would shortly make a choral declaration for Heseltine, news which was philosophically received by Major, though there is good reason to think that, if relieved at no longer needing to employ Howe, he was hurt by the loss of Lawson. Once his protégé, advanced and lavishly praised by him, he was not to have his support at the climax of events. One cannot mistake a subtle falling short of love in Lawson for his former cadet.

Archer tells another story of this day, the Saturday, but one which immediately concerns Margaret Thatcher. Numbers Ten and Eleven Downing Street have a connecting door. He attempted to exit from Ten only to run into Dennis Thatcher juggling five new-found, once lost, golf balls, who beckoned him upstairs. There among the tea chests engaged in a mixture of conversation and packing, were Charles and Carla Powell, Carol Thatcher, Miss Crawford and, sitting on the corner of a sofa, Margaret Thatcher. It was all over. He was impressed that Denis Thatcher had taken over, Mrs Thatcher was low and quiet. She said that she was sorry to go because she would have liked to have been there for the Gulf War. (There would of course have always been something she would have wanted to stay for.)

Archer let her know what he had just told John Major, of Howe and Lawson's coming declaration for Heseltine. Conversation and movement stopped. She was going to say something significant. On his way back would Jeffrey 'kindly drop in and tell John that I do hope his campaign is going well,' her first avowal he thinks, outside the family, of her commitment.

Archer went back to Number Eleven, met Major with his brother, Terry, and repeated the full formal message. It was apparent that the support Major must have been advised of privately, he would soon have publicly.

The irreconcilable friends of Mrs Thatcher find very bitter the fact of her support for Major. They wish to have been tricked, they would like it thought that she was in some way tricked and they like to hint that she has been disappointed by the outcome.

But what she most wanted to do of course was to defeat Michael Heseltine, the name she did not care to speak, the man who by standing had registered the dissent of 168 Conservatives out of 371 for an elected Prime Minister's continuation in office. She had the support of a substantially smaller proportion of Conservative MPs than Neville Chamberlain in 1940!

Right-wing MPs could have been advised to support Douglas Hurd, but she had turned herself almost inside out to keep Douglas Hurd out of the Foreign Office in the Summer of 1989, and had even offered his job to Geoffrey Howe to buy him off. She had chosen to send Major successively to the Foreign Office and the Treasury. In any conflict with Heseltine everyone had to have an option if he should damage her.

She had to have a Not-Heseltine to stand in her name. Tebbit was too rough, Moore was broken, Michael Portillo, like Guy De Vere in the Belloc rhyme, was far too young. John Major, despite the heated argument of 1985, despite a far from secret social Tory inclination, was that contingency choice and had perhaps been so for two years.

Bill Keegan carried a resonating story in the business pages of the *Observer* dated 20 November: 'Mrs Thatcher has chosen her successor ... Why she should choose me of all people to be the conduit of her views – and through the medium of a discussion with a deep-throated person above (of all things) an underground car park, I do not know. I merely report. The designated successor is the present Chief Secretary to the Treasury, John Major. The plan is that after a triumphal re-election in 1991, the Great One will hand over in 1992 or 93 and gracefully depart ...' Keegan's story was printed on 20 November 1988 two years to the very day before Michael Heseltine inflicted what the euphemistic military call 'unacceptable damage' on the incumbent. It fits perfectly the contemporary career pattern of Major and any amount of less specific indications. John Major took it so seriously that he cancelled the booked interviews of the next fortnight as big and bad publicity.

Disobligingly accelerated in the schedule attributed to her by Keegan's source, she nevertheless knew for whom Norman Tebbit should recommend Thatcherites to vote, for whom Francis Maude should help organize a campaign. If, faced with the final contingency, she should find herself ready, what is remarkable about John Major also being ready?

If vicariously through intermediaries, she indeed falls out with him now, Major has the satisfaction that unlike a great roll call of deeply valued and gushed-over subordinates, a roll call which ends with Geoffrey Howe biting the hand which had relentlessly struck him, she falls out *after* office. Any confidence lost is a phantom confidence. After a fifteen-year exercise, Margaret Thatcher's caprice has lost currency. And she has nothing to complain of.

12

A Summing-up

The initial response to John Major's appearance as Conservative leader, was one of amazement, incoherence and high-toned patronage: a 'dim figure' (Richard Ingrams), 'Major (minor)' *Marxism Today*, 'the grey man' (*passim*). This sort of talk reflects a rationalization by the press of their own failure to know about him. Clearly anyone capable of moving shyly through the alcoholic mists, evading a snake-eyed, white-hot press must be a dull little number, one of life's engine number collectors.

Given the nature of London where the Thames is wider than the Rhine or the Missouri, a man from South London (and with the accent still adhering like a shop label on a trouser pocket) would attract extra scorn. South Londoners are of course indistinguishable from one another, alike in their greyness. The press moaned about Major's lack of charisma. They knew who Edwina Currie was, she had charisma.

In this they echoed a wider public. *The Economist*, in its bossy way, had conducted an exercise not long after Major joined the Cabinet in 1987 as Chief Secretary. They set out a polyphoto sheet of two dozen politicians from Mrs Thatcher to any inconsiderable junior at parliamentary under-secretary. Mrs Thatcher, not surprisingly given her office and electric blue presence, scored eighty-seven per cent. Second at eighty-six per cent was Mrs Edwina Currie, beautiful, provocative and charismatic, but only a grade three junior and not that for much longer.

A succession of thains and churls from the departments scored anything between fifteen and sixty-five per cent. The Chief Secretary, a new appointment certainly but a member of the Cabinet in good standing, came last, scoring two per cent.

People talking about 'grey men' and charisma should ponder those scores. Mrs Currie with whom Major had ironically always been friendly, is not grey, she is devoted to publicity in an alcohol-free but addictive way, permanently committed to getting her fix. Ever since she waved handcuffs at a Tory conference when only a candidate, she has been a national figure, to whom tired reporters, lazy photographers and night lay-out men of an unenterprising cast of mind have given unwearying devotion ... She holds no office.

She is nowhere because though diligent, ambitious and intelligent, she first sought publicity by giving emphasis to an inaccurate statement about salmonella in eggs and then lacked the wisdom to back down and say 'sorry'. But she also fell because having queened it in the department from a junior position, she was astonishingly not loved by people in senior posts. Interestingly Mrs Currie, unable to vote in person in the leadership contest, confided her proxy in a senior minister, John Major.

Success in politics needs the steady regard of colleagues, the ability to get on with them or, failing these qualities, a shrewd suppression of all uncomradely elbow-in-eye instincts. Mrs Thatcher on her election was not even in embryo seen as the lady in the chainmail girdle we came to marvel at. She was a rather boring little-womanly Education Minister, disinclined to speak out against the line of Edward Heath which, in a fashion she would make all her own, he deemed correct and immutable. (The impulse of heads of Government to read treason in contrary views is always with us, though Major is probably our best hope of seeing a Prime Minister get through life without paranoia.)

As this life attempts to make clear, Major's presence at a point which would serve for a jump shot at the leadership, was due to his status as an insider. Not knowing about that is for a journalist dangerously self-definitive. If one had asked the people who do not choose party leaders – newspaper readers and writers – who should be watched for as an important runner, then until absurdly late none of the former and very few of the latter would have thought of Major.

An illustration of pronouncement from the depths of unknowing was given in the *Observer* of 13 January by the gossip columnist Henry Porter. I know and like Mr Porter. I have worked with him but can only observe that knowing nothing, he chose to expound it. 'I find it hard not to gape at the screen when I see him with President Bush, Secretary of State James Baker and the troops in the Gulf. Where is the real Prime Minister, I ask? For Mr Major has much of the stand-in about him.

'It is not that I miss Mrs Thatcher but I do miss a Prime Ministerial presence, a sense of leadership perhaps. This is bound to take time to develop even with the help of image makers. It is true that Mrs Thatcher did not immediately acquire that presence of office I am talking about.

'In John Major however one feels that the raw material is simply not there. His voice is too flat, he smiles at the wrong time, he is somewhat plainly dressed and his language lacks turn of phrase and originality. With the possible exception of the early Harold Wilson or the Prime Minister from the twenties (so bland I forget his name), he has the least impressive prime ministerial presence of this century. This is not true of other contenders in last November's leadership contest, Michael Heseltine and Douglas Hurd, both of whom have the potential to look and act like a Prime Minister.

'The media, perhaps aware of its susceptibility to image, has been cautious in criticising Mr Major, possibly in the belief that his achievements begin to outweigh the deficiencies of his presentation. But this is not just about presentation, it is about character and I am beginning to suspect Mr Major cannot grow in the job. I hope I am mistaken.'

If one were teaching journalism, that extended passage would be set as an illustration of what not to do. It is unevidenced, capricious opinion, anchored in no facts and thus dependent on sloppy feeling. It is intolerably snobbish – about speech and dress – the unconscious response of a public schoolboy contemplating an oik who fails to disguise the condition of oik. It proclaims image as superior to substance and advertises further ignorance or its affectation (the unremembered Twenties Prime Minister) as a kind of virtue.

He means Baldwin who saved the Tory party from the near-fascist urgings of the press lords and in a famous speech, denouncing power without responsibility down the ages, stood his ground and won. Only the historically illiterate can affect to have forgotten Baldwin's name.

But at the heart of all this maybug nonsense as it skims the water for its little outing, is the reference to those who do have prime ministerial presence. The two most prime ministerial profiles of our time have been Macmillan, a feeble defeatist who believed he was managing a graceful defeat, and Anthony Eden, that hole in the air, a man who spent a lifetime not living up to the impression created by his appearance.

If Mr Porter really thinks that a mind in slow motion and a dead mouse on the upper lip constitute with the right overcoat and dark felt hat and a bevelled edged voice, the essence of statemanship, perhaps Richard Bellamy is the man we want. In the series 'Upstairs Downstairs', David Langdon played the part of this fictional Conservative politician. He has dark hair greying at the sides, his voice, though gentle, is authoritative with no hint of South London in it. He knows what to do with his hands, has presence all the way, as well as poise, gravitas and dignity. Apart from not existing he is splendid.

Unfortunately it is with such geological ignorance and snobbery that John Major must contend. The fact that the long-serving Chief Whip John Wakeham and the Chancellor Nigel Lawson both adjudged him as beyond question the best whip either had ever worked with, counts for nothing. The running of the spending round without reference to the arbitration of Star Chamber doesn't matter. The fact that, backed by Mr Hurd, he got out of Mrs Thatcher the ERM membership, pursuit of which had destroyed both Lawson and Howe, is trivial. The fact that his party trusted him better or thought him more effective than the two splendid presences mentioned, and did so fourteen years after he was selected as a prospective parliamentary candidate, eleven after entering parliament, is of no account. Henry is emblematic of a string of leader-writers, gossip-columnists and other pronouncers outside Westminster, who knowing as much about politics as the average parliamentary lobby man knows about Astrophysics nevertheless pronounce upon it.

Ask the people who do decide their leader: MPs, and above them chairmen of committees, whips and ministers, and the name would have been in any shortlisting from 1988, a year after entering the cabinet, onwards. It was his emergence as leader so early that was genuinely surprising. The common view about the next leader among politicians ran three years ago like this: Heseltine in crisis if we lose an election or totally foul up, Geoffrey Howe in benign circumstances, over about another year – (before end of 1989), Hurd for any transition after that but for a short reign, keeping the throne warm for either Patten or Major.

Major became at least as papabile as this with sharp people like whips as soon as his first expenditure round passed in 1988 without resort to the Star Chamber. He had not needed a more senior minister to do his diplomacy for him with dismayed spending ministers. He had conducted the talks at party conference in his hotel bedroom. It was jokingly called the slaughter house but the whole point of Major is that he invalidates bloodshot metaphors.

This is a serious political point whose importance has not broadly been well enough grasped. It is trouble enough with a government slipping in the polls, for the Chief Secretary, in effect Minister for limiting expenditure, to get his way with anxious departments and politicians who see their spending as part of the electoral pitch. For any Chief Secretary, never mind a young one in his first cabinet job, to win acceptance of his decisions without appealing to an intermediary, evidences qualities of colleague-management of an exceptional order.

It cannot be said too often that other politicians actively *like* Major; and they have to work with him. Again the words come back: rational, courteous, empathetic, accepting a contrary point of view, endless patience, good temper. These are not grey qualities, they are adjuncts of excellence in a minister, every reason why people close up to what happens would early have put Major high on any runner's list.

The qualities he had shown in the Whips Office: endless pains-taking knowledge of the other side's department, refusal to use this like a bully, personal sweetness of manner, actual fairness and a remarkable reputation for straight dealing, outrun the gaudiest and most exciting personality trait. John Major was elected by colleagues for having been a very good colleague.

Which is not to say that he was without luck. The defeat of Mrs Thatcher at the hands of her MPs, which is what happened, occurred because despite the strength of personality, the element of fear and the manic devotion of many in the associations (echoing admirers of Tony Benn and David Owen), she was perceived as a loser by the two categories which mattered, the voters as recorded in poll surveys and by-elections and the Members of Parliament. They had most to lose from her contagion, and they held the means for her dispatch.

Major's own calculations, once he was thought a possible Prime Minister, have to have been pitched two years ahead; they would assume her continuation up to defeat or victory in a general election. All passing time would weaken Douglas Hurd at sixty, made no difference to Major or Christopher Patten except in so far as events turned out well or ill for each in that time. But because Thatcher did fall – marked as irresistibly unpopular – the change of leader had to be radical, almost radical enough for that change to have been Michael Heseltine.

Major had some personal support from those wanting a drastic humanization of the Tory party, something they trusted to get from him on a basis of extensive personal relationships. All those one-to-one conversations, all that courteous trouble-taking had a reward. But he would also get the votes of the Bloc of Rights, as Lenin would have called it. This came not to a right-winger, which no serious person thinks him, though there is a small bonus for Treasury rectitude and cheese-monitoring, but in his role as Not-Michael Heseltine.

The fact that he handled the media outlets less well and more cautiously than Heseltine (compare for example their respective performances on the question of hiring each other), didn't actually matter. The liberal vote was split with Heseltine, the Bloc of Rights was stuck with Major. Friends and non-enemies combined to help him win, the accomplishment of eleven years near-perfect handling of people. This is not the conduct of a grey man, it flows from the acts of an astute one whose strengths are not, in the grey fashion, wholly administrative or technical. Good departmental minister as he had been, his campaign could not rest on that point. He had sought friends all his political life. He is to a startling degree, short of political enemies. Such as they are, they reflect prejudice above knowledge.

One colleague took a lordly view of the South Londoner with that observation that at the FO they would have to show him on a map where the world was. And Mr Moore of the *Daily Telegraph* wrote an astonishingly patronizing piece effectively intimating that the Tories, having rejected the godlike Douglas Hurd, must make do with this bemused little man and his mousy wife from some godforsaken semi-detached part of south London. If such people insist on voting Tory, what social tribulations one must put up with.

But both of these approaches constitute unprovoked illwill. It is hard to find enemies for whom Major must take important blame himself. This book abounds in the lifelong friends acquired from Brixton onwards: Jean Lucas, Harry Simpson, early parliamentary friends like Robert Atkins, bank people, Huntingdon people, parliamentary people, whips and Treasury ministers. This is not altogether fool my lord.

Yet he has guarded his mouth like an arsenal. Being better able to see a joke than to tell one helps. Since all sharp points enter flesh, there is no man less friended in politics than the wit. Equally this man has held no unnecessary opinions or at any rate has not expressed them. When he went to the Foreign Office nobody knew whether he was a cool or an enthusiastic European. Nobody quite does yet. This was something he would find most helpful in his earliest dealings as Prime Minister at the Rome summit to the evident rage of M. Jacques Delors.

Yet there did exist a rough profile, sketched most impressionistically and expressed as 'economically dry but socially liberal'. As a leader-writer observed, it was the exact mix touted with so little success outside the ranks of bobbysoxing leader-writers, by Dr David Owen. But Dr Owen's last ten years have been spent in painful and sedulous exposition and in perfecting a presence to make Mr Porter swoon. The contrast with Major is a perfect parable. The silences of Major are something for us to think about. They run above and beyond ordinary shrewdness. For it takes either great luck or even greater artfulness to be on hand in November–December 1990 with the exact combination of attitudes which the Conservative party wants in its crisis (and being smart knows that it wants it). The Conservative Party, whatever blunders are committed in its name, however thickheaded many of its representatives may be, is biologically intelligent, the sort of intelligence which passes the A levels of evolution.

The Major rise has always had patrons of course. One thinks of John Wakeham and Nigel Lawson, Margaret Thatcher herself, but before that Tony Barber and before him, Bernard Perkins the council group leader, Harry Simpson the Lambeth Housing officer and Jean Lucas the agent. A lot of able people of some merit in themselves have *wanted* John Major to succeed. They have gone into bat for him, they have recommended him, spoken on the phone, to constituencies in 1974–6 and to a string of voting MPs in 1990.

There is even a touch of geography in his final campaign group. Norman Lamont of Kingston, David Mellor of Putney and Robert Atkins originally of South London were at the front of it. But so were ex-fellow whips and colleagues from the Treasury. Winners collect friends of course and no low motive should be discounted, but there is in the rise of Major a very high degree of other people's attraction to him. And the accumulation of friends based largely on something better than narrow calculation of interests, is a great felicity in a politician.

The man's Prime Ministerial quality had its first test in the circumstances of the Gulf War. He was not the initiator of the British commitment, the glory of which can remain with Mrs Thatcher, but he was charged with what might be called the PR of the war and this he did almost to perfection. The recurring observation of Labour politicians is that it was possible for them, however uneasily, to go along with the party's warlike line because they were spared Mrs Thatcher's corvine delight in battle. The absence of twice weekly calls to arms from a Brown Owl in battledress made life easier.

Major's message to the nation on TV was modest, hushed and a submission to events, not a celebration of them. His parting 'God Bless' was the sort of thing a worried uncle or teacher might have said. It was also very much without mystique, the remark of a member of the crowd happening to be in charge. The absence of self glory and conceit are particularly fitting in wartime where many people are at risk before a politician scratches his finger.

Major accepted the war, approved its prosecution and when it was over went out and told a little joke to the troops. He waved the gift of a Kalashnikov rifle and said, 'Wait till we get argument over the Estimates.' (Ironically Saddam Hussein *is* said to have shot a cabinet colleague.)

Different people have their views about the Gulf War, but even an unequivocal opponent is grateful that someone who accepted the necessity conducted his argument with good manners and a perfect absence of exaltation.

The next reflections on the Prime Minister must be speculative. Given the cards he holds, and the talents he has displayed, how will he conduct politics? How will a man who is not a remarkable speaker relate to the great numbers with votes for whom his one-to-one skills are not available. They may of course be entirely at hand. We haven't yet seen much of Mr Major the television presence. TV is good, neutral or bad without too much reference to tedious old merit. Jim Callaghan was wonderful on television, avuncular, trustworthy and established. Not that Uncle Jim wasn't any of these things, just not as much as it looked on screen.

Major in an election will be what he is in private. The horror for opponents is that against all received wisdom he has charisma, showed indeed in his TV message on the Gulf War. The man lacks Tannoy charisma but rejoices in one-to-one charisma. The country not being made up of gossip columnists, not being in love with striking masterful icons has already recorded unprecedented poll support for him. He is seen as a first citizen, someone very like them but accomplished in office. Barring full impact of the horrors of an economy for which he has some responsibility, it will be enough.

Index